LEADING
ORGANIZATIONS

LEADING ORGANIZATIONS: TEN TIMELESS TRUTHS

Scott Keller and Mary Meaney

Bloomsbury Business
An imprint of Bloomsbury Publishing Plc

BLOOMSBURY

LONDON · OXFORD · NEW YORK · NEW DELHI · SYDNEY

Bloomsbury Business

An imprint of Bloomsbury Publishing Plc

50 Bedford Square
London WC1B 3DP
UK
www.bloomsbury.com

1385 Broadway
New York NY 10018
USA

BLOOMSBURY and the Diana logo are trademarks of
Bloomsbury Publishing Plc.

First published 2017.
Reprinted 2017

British Library Cataloguing-in-Publication Data.
A catalogue record for this book is available from the British
Library.

ISBN: PB: 978-1-4729-4689-8
ePDF: 978-1-4729-4687-4
ePub: 978-1-4729-4688-1

Library of Congress Cataloging-in-Publication Data.
A catalog record for this book is available from the Library of
Congress.

Text design: Scrap Labs

Cover design: Downey Drouin

Cover image: © Billy Currie Photography, Getty Images Collection

Typeset by GS Typesetting

Printed and bound in the United States of America

CONTENTS

FOREWORD

WHEN SCOTT KELLER wrote and told me that he and Mary Meaney had written a leadership book, and asked if I would write a foreword, my reaction was swift and negative. I was confident that a book by two partners at a fancy consulting firm like McKinsey & Company would be packed with breathless hype about novel ideas and claims that these new, unique, and magical insights had helped their clients perform astounding feats—and how these spanking new ideas can enable you and your organization reach the same heights. I was cynical because a discouraging proportion of the 11,000 or so business books published each year claim to have original breakthrough ideas. Unfortunately, most of them—in fact, nearly all—are reminiscent of how the renowned organizational theorist James G. March answered me when I asked him to list breakthrough academic studies in our field. March said that he couldn't think of any, as the best studies and theories usually frame well-established ideas in useful and simple ways or are well-crafted extensions or blends of existing and established ideas. He added, "Most claims of originality are testimony to ignorance and most claims of magic are testimony to hubris."[1]

As I began reading Keller and Meaney's book, I expected the usual boasts of originality and magic. I found none. Instead, as the subtitle says, this book unpacks "Ten Timeless Truths" that have proven to be crucial to the success of the organizations and leaders that McKinsey & Company has observed and advised since World War II. This is the rare business book that follows "Pfeffer's Law," which is spelled out in the book I co-authored with Jeffrey Pfeffer, a fellow Professor of mine at Stanford, and on evidence-based management: "Instead of being interested in what is *new*, we ought to be interested in what is *true*."[2] Yes, the advice here is shaped by the latest (and, especially, the greatest) evidence and experience that the authors could muster. Yet this book is devoted to leadership topics that will "be as helpful to leaders today as they would have been forty years ago, and will be forty years from now." Consider the timeless and vexing questions that Keller and Meaney tackle ahead. Leaders in every era have struggled, and will struggle in the future, with questions such as: "How do I improve the quality and speed of decision-making?" and "How do I make culture a competitive advantage?" Keller and Meaney not only focus on what is true rather than what is new; they concentrate on the ten topics that are most essential to the enduring success of organizations and their leaders.

I was also taken with the "user-friendly" structure, content, and prose in this book. Keller and Meaney help the reader by dividing their insights about each of the "Ten Timeless Truths" into sections on "why is this important," "what are the big ideas," and "how do I make it happen?" The content in each section is carefully curated. On topic areas where I've done work—organizational change, for example—I am struck by the overhyped nonsense and trivia that the authors have elected to leave out. They zero in on the essentials instead. In the chapter on leading successful transformational change, for example, they dig into the few key lessons that matter most—such as how to double the odds of success and the importance of being rational about being irrational. Finally, one of my pet peeves is that business writing and presentations (especially those by academics and consultants) are too often littered with hollow and soul-crushing language. This book has a refreshing absence of what author Polly LaBarre describes as the curse of "jargon monoxide."

After I read the book, and fretted about it for a few days, I realized that Keller's and Meaney's "Ten Timeless Truths" are so easy to digest and so useful because the authors and their colleagues have observed so many leadership successes and failures over the years—and had so much practice passing what they've learned to others. Their journey reminded me of *Profound Simplicity*, a book by psychologist William Schutz that shows "understanding evolves through three phases: simplistic, complex, and profoundly simple."[3] I find *Leading Organizations: Ten Timeless Truths* to be a lovely example of such profound simplicity. I hope you enjoy it as much as I did.

Bob Sutton
January 2017

ROBERT I. SUTTON is a Professor of Management Science at Stanford Engineering School, organizational researcher, and bestselling author. He has written over 100 academic articles and chapters, over 1000 blog posts, and six management books—including his most recent, *Scaling Up Excellence*. He has recently been voted one of the top 10 "Leaders in Business" by the American Management Association (AMA) and one of 10 "B-School All-Stars" by *BusinessWeek*.

INTRODUCTION

Why?

LIKE MOST ORGANIZATIONS today, McKinsey & Company (the firm in which both authors are Senior Partners) is investing heavily in understanding the power of technological advances to help our clients and to enable us to work more efficiently and effectively as an organization. As part of our "Digitizing our Firm" initiative, we've implemented a relationship management support tool we call ClientLink.

Starting in early 2015, client contact information in all of our partners' e-mail address books was automatically cross-referenced with a database of just-released, publically-available business articles from top-tier sources around the world. Based on the company and position of a client executive, the database matched potential articles of interest and sent partners the relevant articles for them to then forward to their clients.

This is a great service both to us as business consultants and to our clients, as it means we all have timely access to cutting-edge, relevant information across myriad sources we couldn't possibly curate ourselves.

Except that we then received these e-mails daily.

At first it was novel, then a chore, then it started to feel absurd. The reason wasn't one of volume (a manageable one or two articles were sent per day), or that the articles individually weren't well written and compelling. It was that one couldn't help but get lost in a blur of buzzwords, frameworks, hype, and contradictory assertions. One day a headline would be akin to "Compassion is Better than Toughness". A month later, "Power is the Great Motivator". Another day it would be "Focus on your Strengths". A few weeks after that, "Stop Focusing on your Strengths"! Then "Kill your Performance Management System", followed by "Performance Management: Don't Throw the Baby out with the Bathwater".

It also struck us that the vast majority of topics being written about were the same as those we studied in business school and those that we've helped our clients with over the past twenty or more years. Topics related to talent and leadership, organization design, and culture and change management haven't suddenly appeared. Yet if you read many of the latest articles about the power of collective leadership, holarchies, or predictive or recruiting analytics, you'd think humans haven't learned anything about organizing themselves in the last 1.8 million years or so of working together.

Stepping back from these observations, suffice to say we are more inclined than ever to lump business literature squarely into Bodleian Librarian and author Richard Ovenden's view that "knowledge is created and consumed at a rate that would have been inconceivable a generation ago... Yet we overlook—at our peril—just how unstable and transient much of this information is... we [need to] choose, more actively than ever before, what to remember and what to forget."[1]

The reason we wrote this book is to provide leaders with a one-stop shop for "what to remember" when it comes to leading an organization—in plain speaking.

Cutting through the ever-increasing, over-sensationalized, and often contradictory clutter of advice for leaders

What?

TO DETERMINE which leadership and organization topics to include, we looked at three data sources. The first was the volume of articles published in the *Harvard Business Review* (HBR) from 1976 to 2016. We grouped the articles into twenty topics related to organizational leadership (versus other topics covered related to specific functions such as strategy, operations, marketing and sales, finance, risk, etc.). Then we analyzed how the number of articles written on those topics varied over time as a percent of all articles published. Our logic was that the lower the variance over forty years, the more timeless the topic (i.e. the topic is consistently written about, versus topics that come and go with the changing times for which there is a higher variance).

HARVARD BUSINESS REVIEW ARTICLES BY ORGANIZATIONAL LEADERSHIP TOPIC, 1976–2016

Relative standard deviation of articles on topic versus total articles in 5-year periods, %

Ten topics that every leader has to grapple with, whether forty years ago, today, or forty years from now

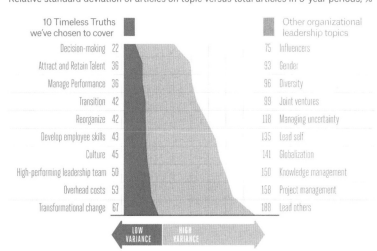

10 Timeless Truths we've chosen to cover		Other organizational leadership topics	
Decision-making	22	Influencers	75
Attract and Retain Talent	36	Gender	93
Manage Performance	36	Diversity	96
Transition	42	Joint ventures	99
Reorganize	42	Managing uncertainty	118
Develop employee skills	43	Lead self	135
Culture	45	Globalization	141
High-performing leadership team	50	Knowledge management	150
Overhead costs	53	Project management	158
Transformational change	67	Lead others	188

LOW VARIANCE ← → HIGH VARIANCE

We then looked at the frequency of queries by consultants to McKinsey & Company's knowledge-management system (as a reflection of what our clients are asking us about), for which we have data going back to the late 1990s. This analysis showed that over 90 percent of the organizational leadership-related searches were inclusive of at least one of the top ten "timeless" topics uncovered in our HBR analysis. Finally, we looked at the history of McKinsey & Company's consulting engagements since World War II (for which we have reliable records) and confirmed that we have relatively consistently served clients on these topics over time.

While none of these sources are definitive by any means, combined with our own judgement they were enough for us to stop analyzing and start writing—confident that the ten topics we've chosen will be as helpful to leaders today as they would have been forty years ago, and will be forty years from now!

How?

SOME BUSINESS BOOKS tend to have one good idea that's explained in the first few sections and the rest of the book is padding. Others cover so much ground that they fall victim to the old adage, "If you write about everything, you write about nothing." We've endeavored to structure the content and create a format so that every minute you spend with us you'll gain a new idea that is punchy and powerful.

The content is organized so that you can digest the book in one sitting, or easily snack on it throughout the day, week, or month. Every topic is divided into three intuitive, bite-sized sections:

Why, What, and How clearly explained in a modern, snackable format

WHY	WHAT	HOW

Why is this important? After an introduction where we define the topic and illustrate its timelessness, we then dive into the top three reasons why this topic is value-creating for your organization. Here you'll find a treasure trove of facts to help you judge the business case for tackling the issue.

What are the big ideas? Here we share the most important insights related to capturing the value for your organization. We do our best to avoid restating what's common sense and push you to think and do things differently as a result.

How do I make it happen? We then get exceedingly practical and share how to apply the insights to deliver real results. We do so by sharing a case study so you can envision the look and feel of the improvement journey, as well as detailing the specific process steps to take. Every journey is structured into the "5As" approach to change that Scott wrote about with Colin Price in *Beyond Performance: How great organizations build ultimate competitive advantage*. Since publishing in 2011, the approach has been proven to increase the odds of success in change programs from the well-known standard of 30 percent to 79 percent.[2]

1. Aspire: Where do we want to go?

2. Assess: How ready are we to go there?

3. Architect: What do we need to do to get there?

4. Act: How do we manage the journey?

5. Advance: How do we keep moving forward?

While the topics are timeless, the format by which we cover each section described above is decidedly modern. Each idea is conveyed first with a Twitter-friendly summary of the key takeaway that leaders need to know. Then the idea is expanded on in a blog-style format that's accompanied by infographics that visually reinforce the key points. Our hope is that the sum of the ideas in each chapter add up to the same kind of intellectual adrenalin rush as a great TED Talk.

And your journey with us doesn't end when you put this book down. Quite the opposite. The same tweet-/blog-/infographic-oriented approach is used in the mobile-friendly website at www.mckinsey.com/LeadingOrganizations that enables you to access further information on these topics, receive the latest insights from McKinsey & Company's organization practice experts, and help shape what topics we tackle next. What's more, the site provides an opportunity to connect with peers who are passionate both about applying timeless wisdom and staying on the cutting edge of leading organizations.

Who?

WE FEEL FORTUNATE to be holding the pen when it comes to putting all of this on paper. In pulling together our best thinking for you, we've drawn on the knowledge and research of many of our colleagues at McKinsey & Company and many other practitioners and thought leaders around the world. That said, we acknowledge that we are simply the beneficiaries of any truly timeless insights offered— these have been forged by the experience and wisdom of innumerable leaders over decades and centuries.

For those not familiar with McKinsey & Company, we are a worldwide management consulting firm founded in 1926. Our clientele includes 80 percent of the world's largest corporations, and an extensive list of governments and non-profit organizations. More current and former Fortune 500 CEOs are alumni of McKinsey than any other company.

As for the authors, Scott is a Senior Partner who has been with McKinsey & Company for over twenty years. He lives in Southern California and is the Global Leader of Knowledge for the firm's organization practice. Outside of work he enjoys spending time with his wife and three boys, playing guitar, exercising, and traveling—a lot (so much so he's been to 194 of the 196 countries in the world to date!). Scott holds an MBA and undergraduate degree in Mechanical Engineering from the University of Notre Dame, both with distinction. He has previously worked as a manufacturing manager for Proctor & Gamble and a photovoltaic engineer with the United States Department of Energy.

Mary is a Senior Partner who has worked for McKinsey & Company for almost twenty years. She lives in northern France and leads the firm's organization practice in Europe, the Middle East, and Africa. Outside of work, she loves her family, reading, and travel. She has a doctorate from Oxford on a Rhodes Scholarship, and an undergraduate degree in Public and International Affairs from Princeton.

Both Scott and Mary would love to hear your perspectives on leading organizations, and can be reached directly at: scott_keller@mckinsey.com and mary_meaney@mckinsey.com. Enough with the preamble. Let's do this!

I. TALENT AND TEAMS

Chapter 1

How do I attract and retain the right talent?

Talent Attraction and Retention:
A TIMELESS TOPIC

IT'S A WELL-KNOWN aphorism in cooking that "Great ingredients make great meals." As a metaphor for business, this thinking can be extended to "Great talent creates great outcomes." Such has been true throughout the ages.

Who did the Catholic Church commission to decorate St. Peter's Basilica, with the desire to make it a potent symbol of papal power? They chose only the most renowned Renaissance artists, including Botticelli, Raphael, and Michelangelo. The cumulative result of their labors is still one of the most famous painted interiors in the world. What did U.S. President Franklin D. Roosevelt do when he learned about the possibility of a German nuclear threat in WWII? He gathered the most talented Allied scientists to work on what became the Manhattan Project, which created a major milestone in the field of nuclear science by harnessing the power of nuclear fission reactions and ultimately put an end to the war.

Let's say you were magically bestowed the role of being the coach of your country's World Cup football (a.k.a. soccer for some readers) team—who would you want? No doubt you'd want the most talented players. Many would feel unqualified for the role and offer to give it to someone who is a better football coach.

Back to the cooking analogy; savvy readers will no doubt point out that someone who is not a talented chef can take great ingredients and make a mess out of a meal (we have proven this many times!). On the flipside, many a talented chef can create spectacular cuisine out of average ingredients. The analogy makes sense in business too; as Katsuaki Watanabe, when he was CEO of Toyota Motor Corporation, pointed out, "We get brilliant results with average people managing brilliant processes...our competitors often get average (or worse) results from brilliant people managing broken processes."[1]

Watanabe's view reflects the reality that there are both cost and availability constraints on getting the best talent, and that having great talent does not mean high performance is a foregone conclusion if the business strategy and company culture don't work together to harness it in productive ways. This brings up the important question of what we really mean by "talent."

We define talent as the natural skill and innate will that predisposes someone to excel at something. So, though you might have the natural skill to be a superior cook—a "sixth sense" or "magic touch" that elevates the food you prepare into a culinary experience—without an innate passion (will) to invest time into cooking and the courage to create new combinations, you'll never become truly talented in the kitchen.

When we talk about attracting and retaining talent, we are referring to how to get the best "raw ingredients" into your organization's human capital "recipe." In later chapters we'll talk more about how to make sure those "ingredients" combine as required to deliver the desired results. Hungry for more? Read on...

YOUR BUSINESS NEEDS

HIGH SKILL HIGH WILL

We define talent as the natural skill and innate will that predisposes someone to excel

Why is it important?
SUPERIOR TALENT IS UP TO 8X MORE PRODUCTIVE

THAT HIGHLY TALENTED employees are more productive than average talent employees is, of course, an entirely self-referential statement (we define talent by how productive they are!). What's interesting, however, is just how much of a productivity kicker an organization gets from them.

A number of studies have looked into this topic. A recent study of over 600,000 researchers, entertainers, politicians, and amateur and professional athletes found that high performers are 400 percent more productive than average performers.[2] Studies in the corporate world reflect similar results, and reveal that the differential increases in proportion to the complexity of the job. In highly complex jobs—those that are information- and interaction-intensive such as managers, software developers, project managers, etc.—high performers are an astounding 800 percent more productive.

Let's put this into perspective. Say your business strategy involves a program of cross-functional initiatives. The program is slated to take three years to complete, at which point customers and shareholders will be feeling the full effects of the work done. Now, with our magic wand, we take 20 percent of the average talent working on the project and replace them with high talent. Practical constraints related to any technology implementation aside, how soon will you achieve the desired impact by affecting just 20 percent of the workforce in this way? Using the 4x number, you'll get there in less than two years. Using the 8x number, you'll get there in less than one.

On the flipside, if your competitors dedicate just 20 percent more high vs. average talent to similar efforts, they'll beat you to market even if they start a year, or even two years later—and that's assuming they haven't poached some of your high performers who are already up the learning curve in the process!

More remarkable (though somewhat less practical) are comparisons of productivity between the top 1 percent and the bottom 1 percent in any given talent pool. For low-complexity jobs (unskilled and semi-skilled blue-collar workers), the top 1 percent are 3x more productive. For medium-complexity jobs (technicians and supervisors), it's 12x. Stated differently, that means a single person in the top 1 percent is worth 12 in the bottom 1 percent. For high-complexity jobs, researchers have declared that the 1 percent comparisons are so big that it can't be accurately quantified!

Steve Jobs, former CEO of Apple, which as we write is the most profitable company in the world,[3] summed up the importance of talent with the advice, "Go after the cream of the cream. A small team of A+ players can run circles around a giant team of B and C players."[4] Management guru Jim Collins concurs: "If I were running a company today, I would have one priority above all others: to acquire as many of the best people as I could [because] the single biggest constraint on the success of my organization is the ability to get and to hang on to enough of the right people."[5]

% PRODUCTIVITY GAP BETWEEN AVERAGE AND HIGH PERFORMERS

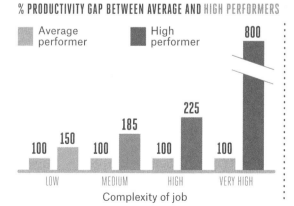

Relationship between quality of talent and business performance

Why is it important?
GREAT TALENT IS **SCARCE**

THE "WAR FOR TALENT" is a term coined by Steven Hankin of McKinsey & Company in 1997, and popularized by the book of the same name in 2001. The term referred to the increasingly competitive landscape for attracting and retaining employees driven by generational transfer: Too few post-baby-boom workers will be available to replace the baby-boom retirement wave in the U.S. and Europe.

Fast forward to the wake of the "Great Recession" a little over a decade later, however, and the War for Talent had become known as "The War for Jobs." Economies were in the grip of financial crises and unemployment rates hit levels not seen since the early 1980s. As a result, there was no shortage of applicants for many jobs. When Walmart opened a new store in Washington D.C. in 2013, it received 23,000 applications for its 600 available positions. This made it more difficult to get an entry-level position at Walmart than to be admitted to Harvard, the Ivy League University (2.5 percent of Walmart applicants made it through vs. Harvard's 6.1 percent acceptance rate).

This buyer's market didn't render the War for Talent irrelevant, however. In fact, in medium and higher complexity positions (for which, as we've seen, higher quality talent has an increasingly disproportionate impact on the bottom line), the opposite was true. Gainfully employed talent became less likely to move to other companies given uncertain times, meaning those that had an advantage going into the crisis only had it strengthened. Further, the significant pressure to reduce HR costs made it harder to discern and win over the most talented.

Looking forward, all indicators suggest the War for Talent will rage on, as witnessed by "Failure to attract and retain top talent" being cited as the number one issue facing CEOs in the Conference Board's 2016 survey of global CEOs (ahead of issues related to economic growth and competitive intensity). This will continue to be true in higher complexity jobs as baby boomers (and their long-experience) exit the workforce and as technological advances demand more sophisticated skill sets.

According to a recent study by the McKinsey Global Institute, employers in Europe and North America will require 16 million to 18 million more college-educated workers than will be available in 2020, a gap representing 10 percent of demand. That means you may not be able to fill one in ten roles you need, full stop, much less with top talent. Further, in advanced economies up to 95 million workers could lack the skills needed for employment. Similarly, developing economies will face a shortfall of 45 million workers with secondary-school educations and vocational training.[6] The battle lines are drawn...

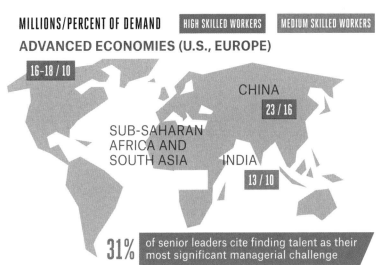

MILLIONS/PERCENT OF DEMAND — HIGH SKILLED WORKERS — MEDIUM SKILLED WORKERS

ADVANCED ECONOMIES (U.S., EUROPE)

16-18 / 10

CHINA
23 / 16

SUB-SAHARAN AFRICA AND SOUTH ASIA

INDIA
13 / 10

Predicted shortage of talent by 2020, by region

31% of senior leaders cite finding talent as their most significant managerial challenge

Why is it important?
MOST COMPANIES ARE
NOT GETTING IT RIGHT

THAT TALENT IS VALUABLE and scarce won't come as a surprise to most leaders. One would assume, then, that leaders are relatively savvy when it comes to figuring out how to win the war for talent. The facts, however, suggest otherwise.

A whopping 82 percent of companies don't believe they recruit highly talented people. For those companies that do attract top talent, only 7 percent are confident they can retain them.[7] More alarming is that only 23 percent of managers and senior executives active in talent-related topics believe that their current acquisition and retention strategies will actually work![8]

Additional facts suggest these leaders aren't just being humble—most companies simply really aren't good at this stuff. Gallup reported in its 2015 survey that over 50 percent of employees in its survey were "not engaged," while another 17.2 percent were "actively disengaged."[9] Related surveys report that 73 percent of employees are "thinking about another job" and 43 percent even said they were more likely to consider a new job than they were a year earlier.[10]

Combine the above with the demographic reality that literally decades of information and experience (in the form of Baby Boomers) is in the process of departing the workplace forever and this state of play becomes even more unsettling. Consider natural-resources giant BP. Many of their most senior engineers have become known as "machine whisperers" in honor of their excellence in keeping important, expensive, and highly temperamental equipment online. If high-quality talent isn't brought on board to replace them, the results could be catastrophic.

Boomers retiring is one thing, but the scarcer top talent becomes, the more those companies not on their game will find their best people cherry-picked by those that are. This will be even more likely in the future, as millennials have far less loyalty to an employer than their parents. According to the Bureau of Labor Statistics, the average worker today stays at each of his or her jobs for 4.4 years, but the expected tenure of the workforce's youngest employees is about half that.[11]

The cost of such turnover is often under-estimated. The more information- and interaction-intensive the job, the more disruption there is to an area's productivity (studies indicate it takes, on average, six months for senior hires to ramp up to full productivity), the more time and money need to be invested in search and onboarding costs and the more your competitors who have recruited your talent benefit from insider understanding of your strategies, operations, and culture.

Stepping back, why does talent matter? Because high value + scarce + difficult = a HUGE opportunity for those who get it right. Let's now turn to what it takes to do so.

% OF TOP EXECUTIVES FROM FORTUNE 500 COMPANIES WHO AGREE THAT THEIR ORGANIZATION:

18% Recruits highly talented people

14% Knows who are high and low performers

7% Retains high performers

3% Develops people quickly and effectively

3% Quickly removes low performers

"Nothing we do is more important than hiring and developing people. At the end of the day you bet on people, not strategies."

Larry Bossidy, former CEO, Allied Signal

Fortune 500 top executives' view of their company's talent management

What are the big ideas?

FOCUS ON THE 5% THAT DELIVER 95% OF THE VALUE

AS WE'VE SHOWN, that talent matters is not a new or surprising phenomenon. We see companies go through cycle after cycle of initiatives to improve how they attract and retain it. Current processes are dissected and compared to best practices and analysis, and analysis is done to determine if the recruiting net is being cast widely enough, if the right candidates are being identified, and if the right cultivation methods are being used. In the end, however, incremental improvements are made while the vast majority of leaders continue to report they don't recruit highly talented people and don't believe their current strategies will change that.

What are they missing? Let's use American football as our example, drawing on the opening scene from the biographical sports film, *The Blind Side*. If asked who is the highest paid player on a team, most people would say the quarterback, given that he is the most central person in executing the vast majority of the plays. If asked who is the second highest paid player, most say the running back or wide receiver, given they work most directly with the quarterback to move the ball forward. And they are wrong. It's the left tackle, someone who doesn't touch the ball at all and is relatively unnoticed on the field. Why? Because the left tackle protects the quarterback from what he can't see (i.e. everything on his "blind side"), which are those things most likely to get a quarterback injured.

What this analogy underlines is that not all roles are created equal: some disproportionately create or protect value, and not all are obvious. For example, the Navy should absolutely ensure they have the best and brightest commanding their fleet of nuclear submarines. Equally, however, they should ensure they can attract superior talent to the role of being an IT outage engineer (the "left tackle" equivalent), whose talent prevents unintended catastrophe for the crew, the environment, and humanity. At the world's largest package delivery company, United Parcel Service (UPS) it's not just about getting the right package handlers, but also the right logistics routing engineers whose slightest adjustments can dramatically affect costs and delivery times to the tune of hundreds of millions of dollars.

In a world of constrained resources, we suggest that companies focus their talent work in the critical few areas where getting the best matters most. Start with roles, not processes (which create generic solutions that don't meaningfully move the needle) nor specific people (that might help you in one-off situations but don't build an institutional muscle to be able to attract and retain the best where it matters).

Be warned that being able to pick the right battles isn't easy—it requires understanding the true economics of value creation linked to specific roles—but that's precisely why it can be one of your secret weapons in winning the war for talent.

THREE QUESTIONS EVERY COMPANY SHOULD ANSWER ABOUT THEIR TALENT POOLS:

How to identify the 5 percent that deliver 95 percent of the value

What pockets of talent most drive growth, execution and motivation today?

How will this change in the next 5 years?

To what extent will the talent you need be scarce or in high demand?

EXAMPLES OF "TARGET" 5% TALENT POOLS:

Logistics routing engineers

Omni-channel merchants

Ship-bound IT outage managers

What are the big ideas?

MAKE YOUR OFFER MAGNETIC...
AND DELIVER ON IT!

MOST LEADERS will be familiar with the term "Employee Value Proposition," or EVP. In plain speak, it's the deal that defines what employees "get" for what they "give." "Gives" come in many flavors—time, effort, experience, ideas, and so on. The same is true for "gets," which include tangible rewards, the experience of being part of the company, how company's leadership helps them, and the substance of the work itself. Ultimately, if your EVP is stronger than the competition's, you will attract and retain the best talent.

This concept is not new in business, yet few companies have EVPs that meaningfully help them win the war for talent. Why? Three reasons:

NOT DISTINCTIVE. HR departments spend months mimicking marketing departments' approaches to determining what employees want. They find what everyone else does—a great job, in a great company, for great leaders, with great rewards. HR departments then recommend that the company's target-value proposition delivers on this—and, as such, it looks like everyone else's who has gone through the same process. Better, we believe, is for companies to stand out on one dimension (whilst not being broken on the others). For example, work for Google if you want a job where you constantly face complex challenges, Virgin if you are inspired by Richard Branson's leadership, Amgen if you want to "defeat death," and Nucor if you want to get wealthy in the steel industry.

NOT TARGETED. It's fine to have an overall EVP that characterizes your organization. More impactful, however, is to have winning EVPs specific to the 5 percent of roles that matter most. For example, if data scientists are key, you'll want to target a value proposition that clearly lets them invent (not repeat), that has a clear and rapid career progression (cross-training), and is tightly linked to having impact (C-suite connected for project scoping and decision-making).[12]

NOT REAL. There was a time when an attractive EVP statement cooked up by HR and pushed through PR had an impact on getting the best talent. This was always a long-term losing proposition, however, as great talent would quickly become disillusioned if reality at work was not as advertised. Today, however, talent won't buy it to begin with. Employees are considered a more trusted source of company information than the CEO (50 percent vs. 38 percent),13 and just as the internet and social media have enabled customers to check if product claims are true, the same is true for EVPs. Sites such as JobAdvisor or Glassdoor have become the job-hunting equivalent to TripAdvisor, offering peer ratings and reviews of what it's really like to work for a company. Your EVP can't just be spin—it has to be real.

Distinctive, targeted, and real EVPs are the weapons in the war for talent. Don't let your competitors win this arms race.

% OF EMPLOYEES SATISFIED: ■ WHEN A COMPANY DELIVERS ■ WHEN IT DOESN'T

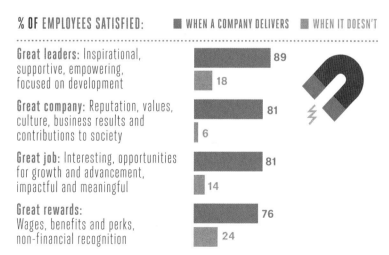

Great leaders: Inspirational, supportive, empowering, focused on development — 89 / 18

Great company: Reputation, values, culture, business results and contributions to society — 81 / 6

Great job: Interesting, opportunities for growth and advancement, impactful and meaningful — 81 / 14

Great rewards: Wages, benefits and perks, non-financial recognition — 76 / 24

The four elements that are most valued by top talent, one of which should be a source of distinctiveness

What are the big ideas?
TECHNOLOGY WILL BE THE NEXT GAME CHANGER

THOSE FAMILIAR with Michael Lewis's book, *Moneyball*, will know that it pits the collective wisdom of baseball insiders (players, managers, coaches, scouts, and the front office) against rigorous statistical analysis in determining which players to recruit. Not to ruin the plot for those who haven't read it, but the machines win, and literally "change the game" forever. Could the same be true in the world of recruiting top talent in business?

When the National Bureau of Economic Research looked into the question it pitted (hu)man against machine for more than 300,000 hires in high turnover jobs across fifteen companies. The result? Human experience, instinct, and judgement were soundly defeated. Those picked by the machines stayed far longer and performed just as well or better.[14] Professors at the University of Minnesota analyzed seventeen of such studies and found that the use of algorithms in hiring outperforms human decisions by at least 25 percent. "The effect holds in any situation with a large number of candidates, regardless of whether the job is on the front line, in middle management, or (yes) in the C-suite."[15]

This is hard to stomach for many leaders. Most believe that pondering an applicant's folder, asking thoughtful questions, and looking into his or her eyes is essential to making critical hiring decisions. Some companies are letting go of such views, however. Xerox replaced their recruiting screening process with an online test developed by Evolve Inc. Since adopting it, attrition has declined by 20 percent.

Richfield Management LLC, a waste company, is another good example. They use an algorithm to screen applicants for character traits that would suggest a tendency to abuse workers' compensation benefits. Since doing so, workers' compensation claims have dropped by 68 percent.

Beyond attracting the best talent who will stay the longest, big data and analytics can increasingly help retain high performers. HR software systems by Workday, SAP's SuccessFactors, and Oracle already gather information from sources such as LinkedIn to provide advanced warning when top talent may be thinking about jumping ship. At McKinsey & Company, we used machine-learning algorithms to determine the three variables that drive 60 percent of our manager attrition—all of which were unrelated to the variables of pay, travel, or hours worked that we had previously assumed.

People analytics are still in their infancy, but gaining speed. Only 8 percent of companies report that they are fully capable of predictive modelling in 2016, but this is up from 4 percent in 2015.[16] If, as a leader, you don't have concrete plans in motion to leverage technology in the war for talent, make no mistake: you are falling quickly behind.

Ultimately, we eschew the idea that only machines will win the war for talent. Consider how IBM's Deep Blue computer thrashed Grandmaster Gary Kasparov in 1997. Yet today, the world's best chess player is not a computer or a human, but human teams playing with computers. No doubt the same will be true in business.

TALENT SOURCING

SCREENING, ASSESSMENT, AND ONBOARDING

RETENTION AND ENGAGEMENT

Examples of how technology is having impact on attracting and retaining talent

Use analytics, online data sources and social network usage to tap latent talent pools

Use surveys, tools and gamification to predict who will perform best

Use analytics to better estimate flight risk and identify individualized retention approaches

20% reduction in time to fill positions

25% reduction in recruiting spend and errors

10–25% improvement in top-performer retention

How do I make it happen?

FOLLOW A 5-STEP PROCESS TO ATTRACT AND RETAIN TALENT

THE NEW LEADER of a major U.S. public institution came into a role with a mandate for change: the department had failed to meet budget for five years running, the press had been having a field day with tales of incompetence, inefficiency, and bureaucracy gone mad; morale was at an all-time low, with key talent leaving in droves. The leader felt that she knew what needed to be fixed. The problem, however, was that she didn't have the talent in the organization to do what needed to be done. And this problem didn't have a quick fix—each division had its own approach to recruiting, all of which were consumed by the vicious cycle of fulfilling immediate needs (the next month). Making matters worse, the attrition came primarily from the higher performers and specialist talent that the organization didn't want to lose. The situation had to change, and fast!

1. Aspire

A TEAM WAS COMMISSIONED to, in the leader's words, "fix the leaky bucket, and fill it with the finest stuff imaginable!" Core members were chosen from each division to be on a task force to meet the challenge, and it was made clear that the division leaders were "on the hook" for a successful outcome. The first step for the team was to rigorously determine what the talent requirements were to enable the five-year plan.

The analysis showed that there were two pivotal roles where more and better talent was needed: key general manager positions as well as critical specialist skills in data analytics. This "demand" view of talent was then coupled with a "supply" view, and gaps identified. The full data set was then reviewed by the senior team who made decisions on where to focus going forward. The senior leaders gave the working team a mandate to be bold if they were to attract such talent.

Aspire
Where do we want to go?

Strategic outlook: Identify the talent implications of your business strategy over a 3- to 5-year horizon

Supply and demand planning: Develop a 3- to 5-year scenario-based forecast of your need for value-added talent, and your likely ability to meet it from the market

Leadership alignment: Gain buy-in from senior leaders on forecasted talent needs and value to business

2. Assess

WITH THE PRIORITIES ESTABLISHED, a deep dive was made into the current situation. What did recruits in target segments care about, and how was the institution viewed on these dimensions relative to their other options? For key roles, where attrition was happening, why was it happening? What was working and wasn't in relation to the approaches being currently pursued? To answer these questions and others, the team gathered data qualitatively, through interview techniques aimed at getting behind superficial, polite answers. Quantitative data was gathered by running a number of predictive analytics algorithms to determine patterns, and analyzing general manager agendas to understand how their time was being spent

The results were enlightening. The value proposition—the promise of interesting work, on-the-job development, and an attractive, flexible career path—was broadly on target. However, the reality didn't live up to the hype. When recruits called their friends hired in previous years, all they heard about was an organization that had gone "bureau-crazy" with little to no coaching. Recruiters were aware of this, but their incentives were to get people through the door and therefore knowingly "hyped" the roles, hoping to meet their short-term objectives. As a result, good talent left quickly while others, happy with the security and relatively high pay, simply adopted a "quit and stay" attitude—they were still on the payroll but contributed little.

Another insight was that specialist candidates wanted a different value proposition than the others, valuing deeper technical development, the opportunity to have some element of "free" time to pursue special projects and a more relaxed and informal environment. And they found the data analytics experts had little patience for "form-filling" or administrative tasks—pain-points that could all-too-easily lead to talent losses.

Assess
How ready are we to go there?

Verifiable baseline: Understand current talent strengths and gaps quantitatively and qualitatively using benchmarks

Assessment of offer: Get employee and broader labor-market input on your employee offer, including operational aspects (e.g. ability to have real impact, leadership engagement)

Drivers of turnover: Determine why your key talent leaves using predictive analytics and qualitative measures

---

3. Architect

BASED ON what had been learned in the assessment stage, the working team recommended a number of changes to the senior team. Two discrete career paths were proposed for generalists and specialists. The role of general managers in large divisions was to be adjusted so that they could play more of a coaching vs. coordination role, enabled by creating lower spans of control and reduced administrative burden. A centralized approach was proposed for data analytics talent, delivering more relaxed and informal events on different campuses and leveraging a much stronger referral program. In specific roles where predictive analytics had shown weaknesses, leaders agreed to follow up with individual "segment of one" discussions with the highest performers to understand their issues and identify a set of immediate actions.

In addition, ten vital leaders who, analytics suggested, were on the verge of leaving, were engaged to help reinvent the employee value proposition for the general manager role. Not only did this give way to better answers, but also acted as a retention intervention. Further changes were proposed to the annual succession planning process (e.g. focusing on pivotal roles), and the recruiting process to make them more efficient (e.g. investing in a web-based platform to consolidate job announcements and candidate tracking).

Architect
What do we need to do to get there?

Magnetic employee offering: Choose sources of distinctiveness for your offer based on what matters to employees and improves operational drivers (e.g. frontline supervision)

Lean recruiting funnel: Reconfigure your recruiting funnel to reduce hiring time and increase intake

Job-design optimization: Remove non-value-adding activities from the jobs of scarce talent to focus their efforts and reduce hiring needs

4. Act

THE LEADER and the top team led from the front in communicating and role modeling the importance of making the target employee value proposition real and vibrant in the organization (e.g. personally attending the newly overhauled top talent leadership development programs). She quickly became known for asking two pointed questions in every performance dialogue: "What are your top 5–7 priorities?" and "Who are your top 5–7 most talented leaders?" Those answering the questions quickly learned that there should be a match between the two!

A Talent Office was created to ensure progress and regularly reported on key metrics such as time and cost to hire, acceptance and attrition rates (overall and for key talent), which was reviewed with as much focus and intensity as operational and financial metrics. Being able to manage talent as rigorously as other elements was a breath of fresh air for leaders. The Talent Office also developed a more comprehensive People Technology strategy centered on finding "hidden markers" in CV screening and attrition.

Act
How do we manage the journey?

Operational excellence: Execute key operational changes in support of EVP and ensure metrics, tracking mechanisms, and governance are in place

Technology roadmap: Determine where, when, and how technology can make recruitment and retention more efficient and effective

Leadership commitment: Ensure a critical mass of leaders are committed to playing their role in attracting and retaining high-priority talent

5. Advance

THE RESULTS quickly started to flow through: employee engagement shot up and attrition declined, especially among the most recent hires. The boost in morale translated into a growing "buzz" on campus, and acceptance rates started to improve. The leader and her team soon found an additional benefit to their new strategy: not only were employees happier and more engaged, but they also became a powerful recruiting source, actively referring candidates and became much more involved. HR capitalized on this renewed energy by launching campaigns "choose who you want to work with" and involving the most dynamic leaders and specialists as "recruiting captains" for key campuses and career fairs. The Talent Office at this point had institutionalized talent transparency across the organization—leveraging an interactive people dashboard with metrics on hiring, quality, fit, and efficiency.

Advance
How do we keep moving forward?

Virtuous recruiting cycles: Use your internal labor market and existing talent as an external endorser and source of candidate referrals

Motivation systems: Align company motives (direction, capabilities, motivation, retention) and employee motives (purpose, importance, recognition and rewards, and belonging)

Monitoring and adjusting: Continuously refresh your long-term view and short-term tactics to meet your aspirations

EIGHTEEN MONTHS LATER, much to the delight of everyone involved in the effort, the organization managed to jump nearly forty spots in the "Best Place to Work" ranking for public sector institutions, one of the biggest increases ever registered. This public recognition also served to strengthen the organization's reputation, further improving their ability to access the talent they needed, especially data scientists who were particularly attuned to wanting the right work–life proposition. Meanwhile, attrition dropped to historic lows, especially among their critical general management and specialist roles. As a final sign of success, the headlines were no longer about the downward spiral of the organization, but talked about the bold new agenda and leadership that were turning the company around.

TALENT ATTRACTION & RETENTION:
AT A GLANCE

⚡ WHY IS IT IMPORTANT?

- Superior talent is up to 8x more productive.

- Great talent is scarce.

- Most companies are not getting it right.

💡 WHAT ARE THE BIG IDEAS?

- Focus on the 5 percent that deliver 95 percent of the value.

- Make your offer magnetic...and deliver on it!

- Technology will be the next game changer.

🔧 HOW DO I MAKE IT HAPPEN?

- Follow a five-step process to attract and retain talent.

  Most commonly neglected element in each step:

  Aspire: Create a 3-5 year view of talent supply and demand.

  Assess: Leverage predictive analytics regarding turnover.

  Architect: Remove non-value added activities from jobs.

  Act: Develop a technology roadmap to enable improvements.

  Advance: Link company meaning to personal meaning.

Chapter

2

How do I develop the talent we need to win?

Talent Development:
A TIMELESS TOPIC

TALENT DEVELOPMENT is central to the advancement of individuals, institutions, and societies, and always has been. If, in the tradition of great science fiction, you were transported back 12,000 years into the Stone Age, you'd better hope that you could quickly develop the skills to fashion flint, antlers, and teeth into tools—and to use them while roaming over wide distances to find food and exchange goods with others. If you were transported back to Ancient Greece, you would probably spend a number of years apprenticed to a tradesman learning how to survive and thrive in that era. If you landed in medieval times as a page on the path to knighthood, you'd be training with huntsmen and falconers, and doing your academic studies with chaplains. Then you'd become a squire, and master riding, shooting, participating in tournaments, and fencing. Having developed the talent needed, you'd be knighted.

In all these cases you would not only need to develop skills, but also the related attitudes and beliefs that enable you to apply them in ways that are valued by the institution and society you've landed in. As the 26th president of the United States, Theodore Roosevelt, said, "To educate a man in mind and not in morals is to educate a menace to society."[1] This takes us back to our definition of talent as "the natural skill and innate will that predisposes someone to excel at something." But don't words such as "natural" and "innate" imply talent is something one is born with? Not in our book. While certainly some are born with a magic touch in certain endeavors, there's no question talent can be developed.

Let's use driving as an example. Nobody is born knowing how to drive. Come the legal age to drive, one has to learn the skill, and adopt the right attitude to do so safely and successfully on busy roads. When we first get behind the wheel, our full attention is required. We need to think about checking our mirrors before changing lanes, putting on our signal before turning, deciding who has priority at a junction, and so on. As we gain more experience, however, driving becomes relatively effortless. We can get from A to B while having a conversation, eating a snack, listening to directions from our mobile phone, and noticing non-driving-related billboards along the way. Once experienced, we often arrive at our destination with little recollection of the actual act of driving there. Now the skill of driving feels natural. The attitude is ingrained. The ability is innate. You're a far more talented driver than you were at the start.

Of course, at higher levels, the "magic touch" factor comes into play and separates the best from the rest. Few, for example, could get behind the wheel in a Formula 1 car and hope to compete against the likes of the U.K.'s Lewis Hamilton. We have already suggested that leaders aim to attract and retain the Lewis Hamilton equivalents for the 5 percent of roles that matter most to value creation—the rest, we believe, are well advised to become "talented drivers", able to do their role's equivalent of getting from A to B quickly, successfully, safely, and legally!

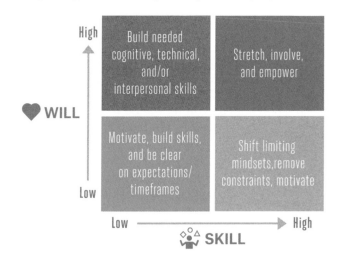

Talent development involves improving the skill and/or will of employees

Why is it important?

YOU CAN'T BUY ENOUGH OF IT, SO **YOU HAVE TO BUILD IT**

WE'VE ALREADY ESTABLISHED that talent is scarce. The McKinsey Global Institute projects a 13 percent global shortage of high-skilled workers by 2020. Even today, in the United States 30 percent of companies have positions open for more than six months that they can't fill. In Japan, 80 percent of companies report similar gaps.

Education systems, while designed with good intentions to meet the economic demands of the modern economy, can't be counted on to help. In many major economies, schools are overcrowded, spending is stagnant, and teacher incentives misaligned. The results of these dynamics are disheartening to say the least. The U.S. Education Department, for example, reports that in spite of the fact that four out of five students now graduate high school in the U.S., more than 60 percent of graduating seniors are unable to read proficiently or do basic math, and as such are poorly equipped for college and the real world.[2] In spite of these poor results, shockingly the U.S. education system is still considered among the best globally[3]—a clear message that companies everywhere can't be complacent.

Add to this the changing nature of work. In the first decade of this century, the job growth in transactional (e.g. bank teller, retail cashier) and production (e.g. factory worker, farmer) jobs was negative, while interaction-intensive, problem-solving, experience- and judgement-based, context-sensitive jobs (e.g. nurses, lawyers) grew at a rate of almost 5 percent.[4] This trend will accelerate further as technology continues to create new possibilities for how to carry out production and routine transaction work with less direct human intervention.

The challenge becomes even greater when you look into the leadership ranks of companies. Senior executives report that over 70 percent of their top 300 executives do not have sufficient skills to capture the business opportunities available to the company.[5] It's no wonder that 65 percent of HR professionals rate leadership development and succession planning as their number one human capital priority[6] and more than 50 percent of employers report they are planning on increasing their investment in developing leaders.[7]

Motivational speaker Zig Ziglar once said, "The only thing worse than training employees and losing them is to not train them and keep them."[8] The reality, however, is that employees who get the opportunity to continually develop are twice as likely to say they will spend their career with their company.[9] Talent development = more of what you need, for longer. That's a good equation for business.

TOP-TEAM PERSPECTIVES ON THE QUALITY OF THEIR TOP 300 POOL

Very strong talent

5%

Adequate talent

21%

Insufficient talent

65%

Chronically short across the board

9%

Senior leaders' awareness of the need for a better approach to talent management

75%

of Fortune 500 CEOs agree that developing leaders is one of their top priorities

Why is it important?

MOST COMPANIES STRUGGLE
TO DO IT WELL

ONE OF THE MOST ICONIC representations of a company's commitment to talent development is the corporate university. General Motors was the leader, developing the General Motors Institute in 1927. The post-War era brought with it two of the best known—General Electric's (GE) Crotonville in 1956 and McDonald's Hamburger University in 1961—and the 1970s saw companies such as Disney and Motorola follow suit. By the late 1980s, there were over 400, by the turn of the century there were over 2,000 and now there are over 4,000.[10] That's more than the number of academic colleges and universities in either the United States or Europe.

Investment in talent development is increasing at an equally high rate. Learning and development spend by companies has grown by roughly 15 percent in the last couple of years to over $130 billion worldwide.[11] The largest share of Learning & Development (L&D) budgets went to leadership development, with 35 cents of every training dollar, on average, spent on training leaders at all levels—from first-line supervisors to executives.[12]

In spite of all of the above, it is evident that companies aren't getting leadership development right: only 7 percent of CEOs believe that their company develops leaders effectively;[13] only 8 percent of Fortune 500 CEOs believe their leadership development programs have clear business impact; 87 percent of leaders want a drastic change in how their organizations develop its employees and over

70 percent of organizations cite "capability gaps" as one of their top five challenges.[14]

Talent development, of course, isn't just about investing in formal training programs that involve corporate universities. Research shows that most development happens on the job, through coaching and taking on new challenges. Yet only about a fifth of employees report getting on-the-job training from their employers over the past five years[15] and less than 50 percent of employees feel their leaders foster development.[16] Moreover, less than half of employers report having formalized frameworks and career paths in place (and only one quarter of these actually track their effectiveness), and just one third of organizations report that their managers are effective at conducting career development discussions with their employees.[17]

Management guru Peter Drucker developed the concept of a "knowledge worker" in 1959. He saw the shift of business and the economy away from success in manufacturing or the ability to make products to success from the ability to generate and use knowledge. "Developing talent is business's most important task—the sine qua non of competition in a knowledge economy," he said.[18] His predictions are proving to be true, and hard for companies to get right.

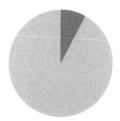

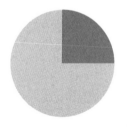

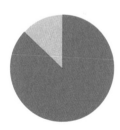

Low returns on the investment in talent development

Only **8% of Fortune 500 CEOs** agree that their company's development programs have clear business impact

Less than **25%** of line managers think their L&D departments are critical to achieving their business goals

87% of leaders want a drastic change in how their organizations develop employees

Why is it important?

COMPANIES NEED TO DO MORE OF IT AS **SKILLS DECAY FASTER**

REMEMBER THE PALM PILOT? Launched by US Robotics, it stormed onto the scene in 1996 as the first pocket-sized PDA (Personal Digital Assistant) that was widely regarded to have "got it right." Such was its popularity that it quickly became one of the most recognized brands in the world. One of the Palm Pilot's unique characteristics was that its users had to write using a "Graffiti Alphabet": every letter of the alphabet was represented in a single stroke of a stylus on a small touchpad. Graffiti took some time to master, but those that did reaped the rewards and were envied for their talents—able to take accurate electronic notes faster than handwriting, often without looking at the screen.

Three years later, Research In Motion Limited's (RIM) Blackberry made its debut with an easy-to-use miniature keyboard enabling anyone to type with their thumbs—no new alphabet needed (which the iPhone later delivered in a touchscreen format). Palm Pilots quickly fell out of favor, and Graffiti Alphabet talent was obsolete.

What if we told you that your employees' skills and attitudes today are the workplace equivalent of knowing the Graffiti Alphabet—within three years, they will be obsolete? While we don't think this is completely true, it isn't as far-fetched as you might think. Consider that, until 1900, human knowledge doubled approximately every century. By World War II, it was doubling every twenty-five years. Today our knowledge is doubling every 12–18 months, and according to IBM, the "internet of things" may soon lead to the doubling of knowledge every twelve hours![19]

This, of course, doesn't mean that half of what your employees knew a year ago is out of date today—not all knowledge is useful knowledge and some knowledge is timeless (if we didn't believe that, we wouldn't be writing this book!). But it does underline how important it is to work out which new information, or skills, may be beneficial for your business to ensure you don't fall behind the competition. For example, a Chief Marketing Officer (CMO) today isn't worth their salt if they don't know how to leverage Hadoop, WordPress, Google Analytics, Hubspot, or Salesforce—yet none of these tools existed when they were in graduate school.

More alarming than knowledge becoming obsolete is knowledge held to be true—that isn't. This couldn't happen to you, could it? Were dinosaurs cold-blooded? Does saccharin cause cancer? Do high-fiber diets prevent it? Are leeches good for medicine? Is Pluto a planet? The answer to all these is "no," yet many have learned (and still believe) otherwise. What might your employees "know" about customers, costs, capital, and risk management that is no longer true, and what impact might this have on your business?

It's clear that employers also need to think of themselves as educators. But how do you make that education happen distinctively in your company?

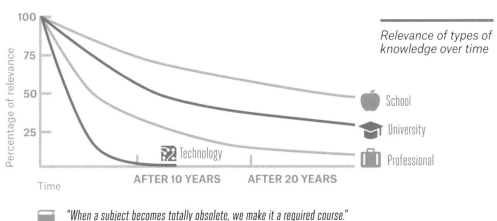

Relevance of types of knowledge over time

School

University

Technology

Professional

AFTER 10 YEARS   AFTER 20 YEARS

"When a subject becomes totally obsolete, we make it a required course."
– Peter Drucker, management thinker

What are the big ideas?
GO FAR **BEYOND THE CLASSROOM** AND THE COMPUTER

THE 70:20:10 MODEL, developed in the mid-80s, is still widely regarded as the best formula for talent development. It suggests 70 percent of knowledge should be built through job-related experiences, 20 percent from interactions with others (e.g. peer learning, coaching, mentoring), and 10 percent from formal education events (in person or on-line).[20] What does this look like in practice? Let's take the example of Stefan, who has recently been promoted to product development manager. As part of his transition, he's been enrolled in the company's First Line Leader (FLL) Development Program. The program is nine months long, with the goal of equipping Stefan with the skills and attitudes he'll need to achieve his stretch-performance goal: to reduce the duration of the product development cycle in his area by 50 percent.

The program starts with a three-day offsite that he attends with 20 others from across the company. He learns that they share similar hopes and fears, which panel discussions with former FLLs help dispel. Based on learnings from case studies, role plays, and group work, he pulls together and presents a plan for his area. He also learns about himself and how some of his deeply held leadership assumptions won't serve him in his new role.

After the first training session, he starts applying what he's learned on the job. He uses a suite of e-enabled tools with on-demand tutorials, gains wisdom from weekly meetings with his mentor (a former FLL, now a high-potential manager, who is playing her role as part of her

Senior Leader Development Program. She also asks Stefan for advice on the cross-business initiative she's leading as part of her own development), and has a virtual monthly meeting with a small peer group for facilitated problem-solving sessions, led by one of the faculty members.

After three months, another training session takes place, this time on leading change. Then there are three more months of on-the-job application with mentorship and faculty-facilitated peer coaching. Then another training session takes place, followed by more fieldwork. The program crescendos at the nine-month point, with the participants, now feeling confident in their roles and excited to lead forward, presenting their results and learnings to the Executive Team.

Stefan's blended-learning journey is a relatively straightforward application of the 70:20:10 model. Journeys such as this are all too rare, however. Only 30 percent of leaders report their companies are good at providing on-the-job training and 25 percent report the same about coaching and mentoring.[21] Participants in formal courses lose 90 percent of what they've learned by the time they go back to their jobs, and formal on-line training sees only 4 percent of companies' on-line courses being completed.[22,23] The winners, however, consistently get it right.

% OF TIME ALLOCATED TO DEVELOPMENT TYPE

Talent development theory and practice

■ Ideal ■ Fortune 500 average

	Ideal	Fortune 500 average	
ON-THE-JOB TRAINING	70%	55%	**30%** report on-the-job training as effective
MENTORING AND COACHING	20%	25%	**25%** report coaching & mentoring as effective
CLASSROOM AND ONLINE	10%	20%	**10%** of learning from formal courses retained, only **4%** of on-line courses completed

What are the big ideas?

MAKE IT **PERSONAL**

WOULD YOUR COMPANY BENEFIT from employees further developing their skills and adopting higher-performing mindsets? Yes, most leaders will say. So what skills do you need to develop, and what mindsets of yours hold you back from higher performance? This question typically gives leaders pause.

At one company, we asked leaders to estimate how much time they spent tiptoeing around other people's egos: making others feel that "my idea is yours," for instance, or taking care not to tread on someone else's turf. Most said 20 to 30 percent. Then we asked them how much time people spend tiptoeing around their egos. Most were silent. This same phenomenon accounts for why everyone can agree that they have a low trust team, but each team member reports they are trustworthy, or why in self-professed bureaucratic organizations you'll be hard pressed to find anyone who identifies as a bureaucrat.

What's going on here? Psychology explains this dynamic as a result of the very predictable, and very human "self-serving bias." This is why 88 percent of drivers rate themselves in the top 50 percent of safe drivers on the road.[24] It's why 25 percent of students rate themselves in the top one percent of ability to get along with others.[25] It's why when couples are asked to estimate their contribution to household work, the combined total routinely exceeds 100 percent.[26] These are all statistical impossibilities of course, and show that in many behavior-related areas, we as human beings consistently have an unwarranted optimism that we are better than we are.

The implication of this dynamic is that the essential first step in any learning journey is to create insight into what a leader can and should change personally (they learn something they didn't know before about themselves). Only once this step is taken can the learning journey continue to the next step of making an explicit choice to learn and grow; putting new knowledge, skills, and/or attitudes into practice in an environment of challenge and support, and ultimately embedding the learning by being a coach for others. [27]

Typically, insight into required change can be created using 360-degree feedback techniques, via surveys, conversations, or both. Note we're not talking about generic feedback against competency models here; we're talking about feedback specific to the skill and/or attitude in question that will drive improved performance. Depending on the nature of the learning program being developed, insights can also be triggered by skilled facilitators prompting personal reflection third-party observation of day-to-day work or simulations and calendar analyses ("you say you are customer-focused, but you only spend five percent of your time reviewing customer-related data, meeting with customers or customer-facing employees").

When development is made personal in programs throughout an organization a deeper institutional mindset is created—one of "My job is to always get better" vs. "My job is to do my best." The former leads to continuous growth, the latter ultimately to stagnation. The choice is yours...

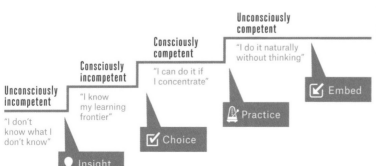

Four stages of development, kickstarted by personal insight

What are the big ideas?
FOCUS ON **STRENGTHS** AND **STRETCH**

MAKING IT PERSONAL doesn't mean making everyone admit they are part of the problem—in fact, it's more powerful to get them to see how their strengths can create a bold new reality.

Consider research carried out at the University of Wisconsin with two bowling teams. First, they were filmed competing with one another. After the game, one team received a video with only their mistakes: they were to watch their gutter balls, analyze what went wrong, and determine how to fix the problems. The other team received a video of only their successes: they were to study their strikes and ask themselves how to get more of them. Both teams then competed again. Researchers found that each one improved—proving watching game tapes is a good idea! They also found, however, that those who studied their successes improved by twice as much as the others.

Why is this? For humans a relentless focus on what's wrong invokes blame, fatigue, and resistance. Focusing on what's right and asking how to get more of it invokes a desire to work together, inspiration, and motivation. Research at work backs this up—employees who are developed using strength-based approaches are 12.5 percent more productive (and have 14.9 percent lower turnover).[28] Further evidence comes from McKinsey & Company and Egon Zehnder's joint research that looked at the mix of "spiky" leaders (those that are exceptional in a short list of competencies and average or deficient in all others) vs. "well-rounded" leaders (very good in most competencies, no deficiencies) in relation to the performance of their organizations. It turns out there are twice as many spiky leaders in top quartile performers than in the second quartile.[29] Taking leadership strengths and making them "spikes" through talent development vs. filling holes pays big dividends.

The secret sauce of focusing on strengths is best seasoned with stretch targets. When someone is already good at something, they don't always appreciate just how much better they can be. How much talent was developed in the 1960s as a result of American President John F. Kennedy's stretch goal of putting a man on the moon by the end of the decade? It's no wonder that when asked to look back at their careers and identify what had helped them unleash their potential, 71 percent report stretch assignments.[30] The adage, "If it doesn't challenge you, it doesn't change you" clearly applies.

We're not saying that strengths are a panacea—certainly strengths can become weaknesses if overplayed, and there are some weaknesses that are Achilles' heels. Also, stretch targets can go too far and then their impossibility becomes demotivating and drives undesirable risk-taking and even unethical behavior. Done well, however, developing talent in ways that ask employees to build on their strengths towards delivering stretch goals is a winning combination—whether in bowling or in business!

Methods for reinforcing strengths

- Create opportunities to use strengths
- Let employees teach strengths to others
- Complement existing strengths with related skills or role
- Apply strengths in new context

Ways to build new strengths

- Deliberately put employees in stretch situations
- Enroll peers to challenge and facilitate risk taking
- Use groups and teams for mutual learning
- Create moments of truth to test new skills

Employees in organizations with strengths-based feedback are **12.5%** more productive and have **14.9%** lower turnover

Methods and rewards of leveraging strengths and stretch

How do I make it happen?
FOLLOW A **FIVE-STEP PROCESS** TO DEVELOP THE TALENT YOU NEED

CONSIDER THE CASE of a leading pharmaceutical company. Faced with major patent expirations on its blockbuster drugs coupled with increasing pricing pressure and a much more challenging healthcare environment, the CEO and top team decided to review their business strategy. After a comprehensive assessment, the team concluded that they needed to exit certain businesses while aggressively expanding in other new, more specialized areas. The catch, however, was the company's existing talent pool didn't match what would be needed to execute the new strategy. After debating whether to change the strategy or invest in developing the needed talent, the team unanimously agreed on the latter.

1. Aspire

GIVEN TALENT DEVELOPMENT was "make or break" to the future of the company as a result of their new strategy, a full-time team was dedicated to the effort. One of the company's rising stars who had recently led their most successful specialty business was chosen to lead the team for a two-year assignment. The team's first task was to comprehensively map out what specific capabilities were central to executing the strategy over the next 3–5 years (the demand view) and getting a clear understanding of the company's starting point (the supply view).

Over a two-month period, the team developed a clear perspective on the overall capabilities required to win: the key technical skills in their chosen specialty care businesses as well as a range of leadership capabilities. In addition to this "top-down" analysis, the team held "bottom-up" workshops with the leadership of the twenty largest countries to pressure-test their recommendations and ensure that they fully understood the talent development needs of each major country and the value at stake. In the end, they narrowed the centrally-led talent development effort to focus on specific technical skills (including much deeper medical skills in the targeted therapeutic areas and a major push to develop their digital and real-world evidence capabilities) and also manager skills to lead transformational change. These recommendations were then discussed and debated at length with the CEO and senior stakeholders.

Aspire
Where do we want to go?

Strategic outlook: Identify the talent development implications of your business strategy over a 3–5 year horizon

Supply and demand planning: Develop a 3–5 year scenario-based forecast of your most value-added talent, needs, and how to meet them through training and development

ROI focus: Work with business leaders to identify the performance metrics they are seeking to improve

Senior leader alignment: Gain buy-in from the top team on forecasted leadership needs, desired competencies, and value to business

2. Assess

IN EACH of the targeted capability areas, the team looked at the top companies as well as their own areas of excellence to develop a "gold standard" that defined the desired skills and mindsets that needed to be built, the management system required to reinforce the capabilities (targets, decision-rights, reviews, consequences), and the tools and technology to enable the capability to be built and have impact. The team then assessed the company's current state against this gold standard using a combination of focus groups, interviews, structured observations, and performance reviews.

The team also assessed the efficiency and effectiveness of the company's current capability-building approaches, looking at the quality and impact of classroom training, online programs, coaching and mentoring, on-the-job development, stretch assignments and rotation opportunities. While there were many pockets of excellence, they also found important gaps: classroom training didn't clearly link to the day-to-day reality of most jobs; continuous feedback and mentoring were notable for their absence; and the company had failed to invest in creating learning journeys that blended the various elements together and linked them to a clear performance outcome.

Assess
How ready are we to go there?

Verifiable baseline: Understand the quantity and quality of your talent strengths and gaps using benchmarks, and identify your biggest development needs

Program evaluation: Understand your development mix and evaluate the quality of classroom and online training mentoring and coaching and on-the-job development

Quality of reinforcing mechanisms: Assess your performance management, career progression, feedback and coaching processes

3. Architect

THE TEAM was now ready to design the needed learning programs and approaches. For each of the target capabilities, they brought together relevant content and learning experts to create nine-month learning journeys that included a blend of face-to-face and online classes, mentoring and feedback—combined with "fieldwork" that directly applied the learnings on the company's most important strategic initiatives. For example, the fieldwork pursued in one of the key therapeutic areas, neuroscience, involved deepening technical and networking skills to enable a new strategic approach for engaging key opinion leaders to be executed. The change leadership course involved numerous elements, including building the skills to develop and manage a portfolio of improvement initiatives while simultaneously ensuring the underlying culture helped versus hindered execution.

In addition to the specific course designs, the team created a plan to develop the needed faculty in order to ensure enough participants could be developed in the required timeframes. A "train the trainer" approach was adopted so that a core set of expert faculty would be augmented by a select group of participants who would ultimately become faculty. The team also defined the selection criteria, identified the candidates to attend the program, and developed a systematic communication and engagement campaign—personally led by the CEO—that shared the strategic rationale for the effort and created excitement and engagement across the business. Finally, the managers of program participants were formally engaged to set expectations and ensure managers' support.

Architect
What do we need to do to get there?

Target participants: Define selection criteria, select initial cohort using multiple sources of input (not just top team views)

Business case/rationale: Communicate the business case, selection criteria, and desired impact to create support and buy-in

High level design: Bring together business, technical, and behavioral experts to design the building blocks of the desired learning programs

4. Act

FOR EACH CAPABILITY being built, the rollout started with a pilot program, after which the detailed materials and approaches were refined and finalized. The programs were then scaled up according to the plan. The early involvement and buy-in from senior and country leadership enabled the rollout to happen smoothly—in large part because they saw that the program would help them deliver accelerated business results. Meanwhile, participants in the pilots created pull for the program by recommending the program to others; they felt proud and privileged to be pathfinders involved in a new way of building capability that simultaneously created significant business value.

In parallel to conducting the pilots, adjustments were made to the company's performance management and other talent management processes to incorporate and reinforce the importance of the change leadership and specialty skills that were being developed. Everything from how employees were recruited and on-boarded, to how they were measured and rewarded, helped to ensure that the prioritized capabilities would become self-sustaining. Two particular innovations involved creating technical specialist development tracks, and making the change leadership program part of the "package" provided to up-and-coming leaders when they were given stretch assignments.

Act
How do we manage the journey?

Detailed implementation: Develop detailed learning experiences linked directly to improving "day job" business outcomes and decide on internal trainers/external vendors

Manager training: Ensure managers are aware of and committed to the role they will play in development and have the necessary support

Formal mechanisms: Re-engineer performance and talent management processes to reinforce strengths and stretch

Compelling story: Communicate the business case, selection criteria, and desired impact to create broad support

5. Advance

IMPACT WAS TRACKED on three levels. First, after each intervention a participant survey and qualitative feedback was carried out. Second, changes in 360-degree feedback and competence evaluations were used to evaluate improvements in participants' technical and leadership skills and behaviors. Third, the financial results that the cohorts going through each program generated over time were isolated. Based on these measurements, the program was continually refined over time. To their delight, the company found that once a critical mass of roughly 30 percent of the target participant groups had been through the learning journey, the language, concepts, and tools started to become "part of the culture" and spread far faster than program participation itself. As such, by the final phases of the rollout, the programs were shortened and enhanced with more advanced content.

Another unexpected result was that, towards the end of the journey, the company realized it had created a new problem for itself: it was now recognized in the industry as an "academy" for talent in the areas it had targeted. As such, competitors started attempting to poach top talent as they came through the learning programs. A number of mechanisms were put in place to mitigate this, including strengthening the employee value proposition for pivotal roles, and leveraging predictive analytics to detect and address early warning signs of potential departures.

Advance
How do we keep moving forward?

Impact monitoring: Measure ROI with same level of rigor as other initiatives and adjust approaches as needed

Virtuous cycles: Use "graduates" to develop next batch of future leaders and embed desired leadership expectations further down the hierarchy and in recruitment processes

Retention mechanisms: Safeguard your developed employees as a scarce asset and use predictive analytics, tracking mechanisms, and top team sponsors to retain them

THREE YEARS ON, the company was well into executing against its strategy, and thanks to its intensive talent development effort, its workforce was an impact-accelerator, not an inhibitor. Results on the business side were impressive: the company had grown its top line at twice the rate of industry-average, with strong bottom-line growth. As for the challenge of being a "talent academy", the CEO summed up his sentiments in saying to his team, "This is a first-class problem to have!"

TALENT DEVELOPMENT:
AT A GLANCE

 WHY IS IT IMPORTANT?

- You can't buy enough of it, so you have to build it.
- Most companies struggle to do it well.
- Companies need to do more of it as skills decay faster.

 WHAT ARE THE BIG IDEAS?

- Go far beyond the classroom and the computer.
- Make it personal.
- Focus on strengths and stretch.

 HOW DO I MAKE IT HAPPEN?

- Follow a five-step process to develop the talent you need.

  Most commonly neglected action in each step:

  Aspire: Focus on capabilities needed to deliver the strategy.

  Assess: Understand the efficacy of current approaches.

  Architect: Involve business leaders (not just HR) in design.

  Act: Ensure managers of participants have a role.

  Advance: Link learning to retention mechanisms.

Chapter

3

How do I manage performance to unlock our full potential?

Performance Management:

A TIMELESS TOPIC

YOU'RE A POLITICIAN with great ambition, so much so that you are considering a run for Prime Minister. You've got plenty of experience in public service to draw on, but want to learn more about the role and how to be successful. You proceed to have a look on-line, reading through summaries of the various texts available for purchase. One in particular catches your eye. It talks explicitly about the role of the Prime Minister. It details a process for defining departments, allocating responsibilities among them, and creating procedures to help them stay connected to their work. It also describes in detail how to reward performance through promotion, compensation, and recognition, as well as the use of fines, removal from office, and reprimand when things aren't going well. "Perfect," you think to yourself. Then you look at the title: *The Officials of Chou*, and realize it was written in 1100 B.C.![1] Hmmm, perhaps not the best place to start...

While a 3,000-year-old manuscript from China's Chou Dynasty may not suit our needs in the scenario above, its existence proves that performance management has long been part and parcel of managing organizations. By performance management we mean the process by which individual performance expectations are set, in alignment with company goals, and progress against those expectations is supported, encouraged, evaluated, and rewards and consequences administered accordingly.

The modern history of performance management traces its roots back to the Industrial Revolution. The first industrial application of a merit-based rating system was introduced in cotton mills in Scotland in the early 1800s. Wooden cubes of different colors indicating different degrees of merit were hung over each employee's work station. As performance changed, so did the appropriate wooden cube.[2] By the early 1960s, it was estimated that more than 60 percent of American organizations had some kind of established performance management system[3] and, by the 1980s, virtually all large companies had some formal process in place.

Over the last three decades, practices have evolved to strike a better balance between being backward- and forward-looking, and to complement financial rewards and consequences with a fuller set of motivators. This period has also seen the rise—and the beginning of the fall—of time-intensive, forced-ranking approaches used to differentiate performance. The goal of these approaches was to increase employee motivation to excel, but the cumulative result has been the opposite, as the actions of iconic companies such as GE and Microsoft have acknowledged through their wholesale abandonment of them.

Today, headlines such as "The End of Performance Management"[4] would have you believe that, in spite of three millennia of evolution, this practice may become extinct. We disagree. Let us explain why...

COMPANY GOALS

INDIVIDUAL EXPECTATIONS

REWARDS AND CONSEQUENCES

SUPPORT/ENCOURAGE/EVALUATE

Performance management is the process that links company goals to individual performance expectations and motivates delivery against those expectations

Why is it important?

DONE WELL,
IT **DELIVERS RESULTS**

WHY DOES PERFORMANCE management matter? American College Football coach Mick Delany sums it up in his inimitable way, "Any business or industry that pays equal rewards to its goof-offs (low performers) and eager beavers (high potentials) sooner or later will find itself with more goof-offs than eager beavers."[5] Case closed? It's a strong argument, but in fact there are far more reasons to ensure your organization is characterized by good performance management.

Management guru Peter Drucker is in many ways the father of modern performance management. In his 1954 book, *The Practice of Management*, he popularized the process of what he called "Management by Objectives" (MBO). MBO starts with collaboratively translating your strategy into objectives that can be cascaded down the hierarchy, answering the employee question, "What am I supposed to achieve, and why?" It then measures progress against a desired outcome, answering the employee question, "How am I doing?" By prescribing the desired outcome but not the specifics of how to achieve the outcome, it empowers employees to bring their full creativity and capability to bear. Moreover, it provides tools and guidance as to how employees can progress faster towards better and more sustainable outcomes than they otherwise might, answering the employee question, "How can I improve?" Finally, it provides rewards and recognition and administers consequences fairly based on the achievement of the relevant objectives, answering the employee question of "What does this mean for me?" In total, the process is meant to create a fair and transparent "cause and effect" result commensurate to each employee's part in executing the business's strategy.

At this level, it's not hard to see why the numerous well-regarded companies, such as Hewlett-Packard (HP), DuPont, and Intel, adopted and adapted Drucker's model and found it to be an important ingredient in their success.[6] It's also no surprise that researchers have found that when leadership have high commitment to this type of performance management, their efforts deliver an average gain in productivity of 56 percent vs. 6 percent when commitment is low.[7] In our research, we've seen that companies that achieve top quartile accountability using such approaches are 1.9 times more likely to demonstrate above-median profits.[8]

Clearly, then, the business case for good performance management is strong. But you knew that. As do the 94 percent of leaders who, when surveyed, agree that it is an important driver of business performance.[9] And the basics aren't rocket science—in fact, when asked how to execute a strategy, most leaders recite a remarkably similar formula to the four elements described above.[10] So why is it that in 2015 CEOs ranked "improving our performance management processes" as their most important human capital strategy?[11] For that, you'll have to read on...

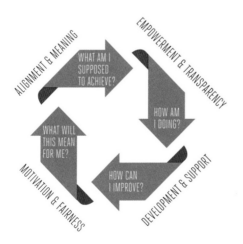

OF LEADERS BELIEVE
PERFORMANCE MANAGEMENT
DRIVES BUSINESS PERFORMANCE

ABOVE-MEDIAN PROFITS
ARE ACHIEVED BY ORGANIZATIONS
WITH **HIGH ACCOUNTABILITY**

Anatomy of a well-functioning performance management process and its benefits

Why is it important?
WHAT MOST COMPANIES ARE DOING **ISN'T WORKING**

A RECENT DILBERT CARTOON (the comic strip by Scott Adams that portrays workplace mismanagement in a humorous manner) starts with the pointy-haired boss stating to an audience of engineers, "Every company needs goals. We have division goals, department goals, district goals, personal goals, and affiliate goals. You will attend a four-hour training session on how to write goals. Every week you will report on how you are doing compared to your goals. Those goals will be entered into a giant database..." Dilbert, one of the engineers, interrupts with a question, "Won't the size and complexity of the database make it impossible to know what's really happening?" The pointy-haired boss deadpans back, "Yes, that's why your raises will be based on what you look like."

This satirical portrayal of office life reveals the tragedy of contemporary performance management. It's no longer what Drucker would call a "practice of management," but instead it's typically a complex, bureaucratic process administered by Human Resources. The result? In most companies it does not improve performance. If anything, it lowers it.

How do we know? Because only 29 percent of employees report that the current approaches effectively support the delivery of business objectives, 73 percent of employees report they have not seen practices move from a focus on paperwork to a focus on conversations, and only 8 percent of employees believe that their managers are highly skilled at ensuring that evaluations are fair and equitable. Most telling, however, is that 89 percent of employees believe their performance would significantly improve if their company's approach to performance management were changed.[12,13]

None of this is happening by intention, of course. Multiple factors have contributed to this situation becoming the reality. The sheer size of companies has prompted the adoption of a homogenous approach in the spirit of fairness, creating a proliferation of metrics, and making the absolute time spent on the process enormous. The advent of the matrix organization, aimed at capturing economies of scale and skill, has made it far more difficult to trace cause and effect. An increasing desire not just to measure and manage outcomes but also leading indicators such as attitudes, behaviors, and potential has further proliferated metrics and watered down the importance of any one metric in the process. Advances in technology that enable massive amounts of data to be stored and accessed have increased the bureaucracy of inputs and complexity of outputs, and caused people to lose touch with "why?" Finally, increasingly litigious societies have resulted in the need for excessive documentation and organizing the process around the once-a-year event of adjusting compensation versus an on-going dialogue.

The Dilbert cartoon we opened with is amusing. Considering that the costs of today's performance management approaches are estimated at $35 million a year for a company of 10,000 employees,[14] the reality is just plain depressing. Fortunately, this isn't the end of the story...

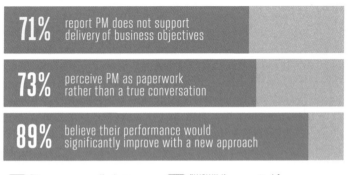

71%	report PM does not support delivery of business objectives
73%	perceive PM as paperwork rather than a true conversation
89%	believe their performance would significantly improve with a new approach

Perceptions of performance management in practice

"Yes, everyone really does hate performance reviews"
Wall Street Journal

"WOW!! I'm so excited for my performance appraisal today..."
No one ever said

MORE IS KNOWN ABOUT WHAT WORKS THAN EVER BEFORE

YOU'VE BEEN EYEING that leather sofa for the family room, but at full price it's $3000. That just feels like a lot to pay for a couch, so you're sticking with what you've got. Meanwhile, at the car dealership you're negotiating the purchase of a new family car. The car itself is $40,000, but they've said they'll throw in leather seats, which would normally cost an extra $6,000 for half price. Sold!

Why are we happy to spend a small fortune during sales, but reluctant to pay so much for full-priced goods? It's the same reason most people would be fine with taking a pencil from the office for their child to use at school, yet be shocked if they heard that someone raided the petty cash drawer to buy their kid's school supplies. The answer comes from cognitive psychology—as humans we are "predictably irrational;" i.e. we have predictable modes of thinking that don't abide by what would generally be considered "rational."

This is important to performance management because, during the 1950s, when Peter Drucker wrote about MBOs, the predominant branch of psychology was behaviorism—your environment, and in particular rewards and consequences for actions, drive the behaviors you choose. Cognitive psychology, which came to prominence only in the late 1960s, looked beyond stimulus and response into the examination of the mental processes that underlie our decision-making—revealing that humans don't always behave rationally. This finding dramatically altered economic theory, creating the branch of behavioral economics, and is ripe for the picking to improve how performance is managed.

Take for example the finding that small, unexpected rewards have a more significant impact on motivation versus annual bonuses, which themselves have little impact except in relation to tasks that consist of basic, mechanical skills.[15] Or the finding that intrinsic motivation (meaning, autonomy, mastery) drives higher performance than extrinsic motivation (financial or emotional rewards and punishment)—and actually diminishes when extrinsic motivators are increased.[16] Add to these the findings that we discuss elsewhere in this book such as how employee involvement during the process creates disproportionately more commitment to the outcome (see Chapter 9), how focusing on leveraging strengths creates far more energy and enthusiasm than addressing weaknesses (see Chapter 2), and that if employees feel the *process* isn't fair their demotivation is stronger than if they feel an *outcome* is unfair (which we will discuss later in this chapter).

These learnings account for why Dan Pink, in his best-selling book, *Drive*, famously proclaimed, "Carrots and sticks are so last century."[17] We only partially agree. In our view, the basics were never broken—just strayed from over decades. The secret sauce lies not in abandoning the behaviorist approaches (pushed by those professing that the end of performance management is upon us), but in augmenting them with techniques derived from the cognitive view. Like the yin and the yang, the seemingly opposite approaches can reinforce one another to fully unlock latent motivation in the workforce.

% OF RESPONDENTS ANSWERING "EXTREMELY" OR "VERY EFFECTIVE"

FINANCIAL INCENTIVES
(cash bonuses, base salary increase, stock options)
49%

NON-FINANCIAL INCENTIVES
(praise, attention, opportunities for further impact)
64%

"*Human beings have an innate inner drive to be autonomous, self-determined, and connected to one another. And when that drive is liberated, people achieve more and live richer lives.*"

Dan Pink, *Drive: The Surprising Truth About What Motivates Us*

Effectiveness of financial and non-financial incentives

What are the big ideas?

HARMONIZE COMPANY AND EMPLOYEE MOTIVES

THE HISTORY of parenting in Western societies is instructive for performance management. For the majority of the twentieth century, an *adult-centered* approach to parenting was the norm. This approach resembled traditional performance management to the extent it held that parents should exert their legitimate authority over their children: set goals, guide and direct their child's development, and administer consequences to improve behavior. Too many children brought up under these conditions found themselves entering adulthood feeling resentment, lacking in confidence and self-esteem, and too often trapped into life paths for which they have little passion. So they fought back.

Enter the era of *child-centered* parenting. In this model, children aren't lumps of clay to be molded, but are free to be active in their own development and learning. Parents are meant to be "a guide on the side" rather than an all-knowing "sage on the stage." Doing so, the promise has been that children will grow up with a strong sense of individuality, creativity, and purpose in their lives—and as such achieve their full potential. Unfortunately the results haven't lived up to the promise, with too many children ending up narcissistic, entitled, and lacking the capacity to persevere and cope with difficulty.[18]

In a similar fashion, the pendulum has swung from *employer-centric* approaches to performance management to *employee-centric* approaches. Filled with good intentions, business leaders and HR professionals are now swinging the pendulum to no performance ratings, no peer comparisons, just anxiety-free continuous development conversations to help employees pursue their passions. We fear that these leaders, and their employees, will end up just as disappointed as the parents and children who swung the analogous pendulum mentioned in the example above.

We urge companies to solve for company and employee goals simultaneously. Goals should be set with career aspirations and passions taken into account (employee-centric), but they also need to drive forward the priority business strategies of the company (employer-centric). Individual strengths should be recognized and developed and support given to achieve goals (employee-centric), but skills built should be part of a broader institutional capability-building aspiration and should reinforce company values and culture (employer-centric). Rewards should be fair and meaningful, and include the potential for shaping one's career path (employee-centric), but incentives must reflect achievement of outcomes, retain high performers, and not let lower performers damage results or block the career progress of those more talented (employer-centric).

As companies making employee-centric overhauls to their performance management systems are in the early stages of change, only time will tell if our parenting analogy will hold true. In the meantime, we are confident those that pursue the "middle way" described above won't be disappointed.

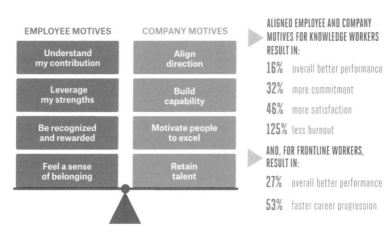

EMPLOYEE MOTIVES	COMPANY MOTIVES
Understand my contribution	Align direction
Leverage my strengths	Build capability
Be recognized and rewarded	Motivate people to excel
Feel a sense of belonging	Retain talent

ALIGNED EMPLOYEE AND COMPANY MOTIVES FOR KNOWLEDGE WORKERS RESULT IN:

16% overall better performance

32% more commitment

46% more satisfaction

125% less burnout

AND, FOR FRONTLINE WORKERS, RESULT IN:

27% overall better performance

53% faster career progression

Examples of company and employee motives –and the rewards that come from balancing them

What are the big ideas?
SOLVE FOR **FAIR PROCESS**

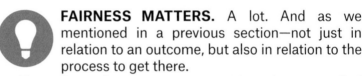 **FAIRNESS MATTERS.** A lot. And as we mentioned in a previous section—not just in relation to an outcome, but also in relation to the process to get there.

To explain what we mean, consider what are called "Ultimatum Games": Player A is given a sum of money. Let's say US$10. Player A is to share the money with player B, and is free to determine what split of the money will be offered. Player B can then accept or reject the offer from player A. If accepted, both players get to keep the agreed share of the money. If player B disagrees, no one gets any of the money. If the money is split equally, in 100 percent of cases player B accepts the terms. But what if player A offers to keep $7.50 for themselves and give $2.50 to player B? In these cases, more than 95 percent of the time the offer is rejected. To punish player A for being unfair, player B forgoes the opportunity to make money. This isn't just a function of small sums, either. The same dynamic has proven to be true with the equivalent of two weeks of pay.[19]

Is it fair for high performers who create disproportionate value for a company to be rewarded more than average or low performers? Most would say yes. Is it fair to smart, hard-working, well-intentioned employees that lazy, ill-intended employees who make poor decisions are not dealt with? Most would say no. This line of thinking is what led to the rise of forced rankings in performance management. Pioneered over the twenty years Jack Welch ran GE (during which time earnings increased 28-fold), the approach is used by over half of the Fortune 500.[20] It requires a portion of employees (typically following a bell curve) to be ranked in specific performance categories—for example, "top," "good," "fair," "poor," "unacceptable." Rewards and consequences are then commensurate with one's rating.

While on paper forced ranking seems fair, in practice it has proven quite the opposite. Rankings are seen as political exercises by leaders fueled by employees' self-promoting behaviors. Risk-taking is avoided, creativity squashed, and individual survival put ahead of collaboration and company success. Because of this, an estimated 10 percent of Fortune 500 companies, including Adobe, Accenture, Gap, Medtronic, Deloitte and, yes, GE, have all very publically abandoned the process.[21] Some have gone so far as to abandon performance rankings all together.

This has us concerned that in a few years we'll be back to the same state that prompted the rise of stacked rankings to begin with. We believe people aren't against being evaluated and, in fact, they *want* to know where they stand. They just want the process to be fair. They want a process that differentiates without false precision, that is both forward- and backward-looking, that happens far more frequently than once a year (but not so much as to create feedback fatigue), that involves an honest, two-way conversation, that is based on more data and input than just the boss's view, considers not just what was achieved, but also how and links rewards and consequences to performance.

Easier said than done...yet easier to do once said!

FAIR PROCESS

- Real differentiation without false precision
- Backward- AND forward-looking
- Continuous feedback without creating fatigue
- Honest two-way conversations
- Diverse inputs (data, customer/peer input, etc.)
- Outcomes (what) and behaviors (how) both valued
- Rewards/consequences linked to performance

Important features of a fair performance management process

What are the big ideas?

PUT **SKILLS FIRST**, NOT SYSTEMS AND DATA

AT THE STROKE OF MIDNIGHT on May 20, 2002, East Timor became a fully independent country after three years of UN presence. China was the first country to establish diplomatic relations and, in doing so, upped its pledge of reconstruction aid to the country to US$16 million. While this and other aid has no doubt been put to good use, when one of the authors of this book, Scott, an avid traveler, visited the country some five years later he heard a different story. His guide told him the reality on the ground hadn't changed since the birth of the new nation, primarily due to the poor transport infrastructure. Later that day they came across a field full of bulldozers, compactors, jaws, and all manner of heavy construction equipment ideal for road-making. The field was overgrown, the equipment rusting and a few local children used it as a giant yellow playground. "What's all this?" Scott asked. "Equipment donated from China," came the response. "What's wrong with it?" His guide replied, "Nothing, but no one trained us how to use it."

Talk to many HR professionals today about performance management in their organizations and they'll typically share not only an employee-centric view that moves towards no ratings, but also one that is full of technological bells and whistles. New human resource management (HRM) software makes things more accurate and streamlined, and leads to better decisions and feedback, they'll say. Social and mobile recognition tools will enable more precise, frequent, and motivating feedback. Predictive analytics on data from wearable technology will reveal new insights into how to do the job, and coach the job, well. And so on.

While technology is no doubt bringing positive changes, we suggest leaders direct the majority of their focus to skills, not systems and data, or we fear an East Timor-like investment in technology will bear little fruit on the ground. For example, no amount of technology is needed to make leaders good at helping employees set stretch goals that are motivating to them, conduct a two-way performance dialogue that identifies strengths and helps employees see how they can be used to overcome weaknesses and improve performance, and know how best to tailor messages and consequences in ways that will maximize motivational impact.

The leaders who are good at these things are probably already doing them today, and those that aren't won't change because of a new system. Recent studies of companies newly operating without ratings reveal that performance conversation quality declines by 14 percent, managers spend on average ten fewer hours having informal performance conversations, top performers' satisfaction with pay differentiation decreases by 8 percent, and overall employee engagement drops by 6 percent.[22] The root causes of these negative impacts all relate to managers' discomfort and lack of skill in working without old crutches (e.g. many don't know what to talk about if not justifying a rating and commiserating about the system that created it). And here our chapters on performance management and talent development collide!

1) Understanding the PM process
2) Setting stretch goals
3) Gauging performance
4) Conducting performance dialogues
5) Prioritizing improvement actions
6) Thinking both short and long term
7) Holding people accountable
8) Tailoring rewards and consequences

EXPECTATIONS
FEEDBACK
SUPPORT
REWARDS/CONSEQUENCES

Example capabilities required to manage performance effectively

How do I make it happen?

FOLLOW A **FIVE-STEP PROCESS** TO PUT IN PLACE THE RIGHT APPROACH

THE LEADERS OF a European insurance company felt great about their strong market leadership, healthy financial performance, highly respected brand, and deep customer focus. They were shocked, therefore, to find out in an employee survey that the motivation scores of the workforce, in particular those of middle and lower management, were in the fourth quartile. Digging deeper into the data they saw that the issues were centered on the performance management process. In particular, reviews and the link between performance and rewards/consequences were seen to be broken. The senior team rightly worried that were this to continue then all that they were feeling good about could quickly slip away, and therefore embarked on an effort to transform the performance management process.

1. Aspire

THE FIRST ORDER of business was for the CEO and senior team to fully align on the overall objective, and the guiding principles for the work to come. In order to facilitate these decisions, a working team pulled together a high-level set of choices for the top team to discuss. For each choice, where the company was today on each dimension was clearly laid out, as well as what other peer companies had chosen and what the relative trade-offs were. When the time came for discussion, getting alignment on the overall objective was relatively straightforward: everyone agreed that this wasn't just about fixing the pain points identified in a survey, but about ensuring the performance management process was unlocking business benefits and enabling them to attract and retain talented employees. They also agreed that the administrative burden needed to be kept to a minimum.

Working through the principles sparked more debate, however. How much weight should be given to past performance vs. future development? How should stretch versus base targets be used, if at all? Should ratings be used and, if so, how much differentiation in ratings should be forced into the system? What role should non-financial rewards and recognition play versus financial compensation? Who should drive the review process, the manager or the employee? How broad should the inputs to the process be? How frequently should performance management conversations happen, and what would their relationship with annual compensation decisions be? All of these questions and more were discussed and ultimately decided upon— giving the working team a clear direction for the next phase.

Aspire
Where do we want to go?

Strategic objectives: Clearly define key objectives for the performance framework in line with aspirations and business demands

Design choices: Address key questions in strategy and design, target setting, performance evaluation, and consequence management

Leadership model: Distil the leadership implications of all of the above into clear expectations of leaders

2. Assess

THE WORKING TEAM then took the decisions made on the high-level principles and dug deeper into the current state—looking beyond what was happening into why it was happening for the areas in need of change. A closed-file review of the last three years of ratings showed that in the company's five-point rating scale, 95 percent of managers had been rated "above average" and that the rating of "below average" was literally never used. Digging into why, the team discovered that the pride taken in the friendly, approachable, "family" culture made leaders feel like a low rating was against the values of the company—everyone had something to offer (and firing someone for low performance was unheard of). What's more, those with average ratings were harder to move into other areas, so giving subordinates such a rating was essentially sentencing oneself to forever work with lower performers. The working team quickly realized any changes couldn't just take the form of process, but also needed to include a substantial shift in managers' mindsets and capabilities to motivate employees, to coach and develop through performance dialogues, and to be willing to differentiate and apply real consequences (both positive and negative) based on performance.

The findings were reviewed with the senior team, who themselves had to face the fact that feedback had not just come from middle managers lower down in the organization, but also from their direct reports—for things to change, they had to change. Before moving to the next phase, the top team engaged in a remarkably open discussion about how they themselves avoided tough conversations, worrying that these could irreparably damage relationships. They also acknowledged for the first time that they didn't really know what real performance dialogues looked like, and how—despite talking a lot about how important an open and direct culture was—theirs was far from it.

Assess
How ready are we to go there?

Process diagnostic: Analyze processes for efficiency and effectiveness against benchmarks and best-practice examples

Feedback review: Conduct a closed-file review of performance appraisals to determine strengths and weaknesses of current approach

Change readiness: Determine gaps between current and desired mindsets and skills

3. Architect

ARMED WITH the above, the working team went to work on the detailed design of the new approach, including all of the capability building and change management that would be required to make it work in practice. Through the course of multiple working sessions that included significant input from all of the major business units and representation from different levels of the organization, the team settled on a four-part model. The first part, answering the question, "What do I need to achieve?", set both base and stretch targets based on one's strengths. The second part, "How am I doing?", would regularly assess team and individual performance. The third, "How can I improve?", prioritized improvement opportunities for both the short and long term. The final part, "What does this mean for me?", would hold people accountable and ensure real, differentiated rewards for good and bad performance.

Each step of the process was accompanied by a set of tools, capability-building modules, and a delineation of helpful versus harmful mindsets. For example, for the first step, leaders were equipped with tools that ensured no more than 5–7 performance indicators would be part of the process (previously there were twenty or thirty a manager was held to, making each individual indicator largely meaningless), and that the link to the company's overall business objectives was specified. Capability-building modules were created to teach leaders how to identify strengths and use them to set tough but doable stretch goals. The existing mindset of "I need to get into the detail or I will lose control" was called out and an alternative, more helpful mindset of "the more I empower my team, the more likely they'll outperform" suggested, with evidence to back up its efficacy.

Architect
What do we need to do to get there?

Detailed process design: Outline the end-to-end process across the four elements, testing for simplicity and clarity

Stakeholder engagement: Map stakeholders and plan how to bring them on board with aspirations and new process design

Mindsets & capabilities: Flesh out plan to shift to needed mindsets and behaviors

4. Act

ONCE THE new approach was designed, it was piloted in two areas. First the top team participated in a series of workshops where they simulated a full year's performance cycle in order to fully understand and get upskilled in the new system. As part of the process, actors role-played good and bad performance conversations, and pushed leaders well out of their comfort zone to practice what the new dialogue should look like. At various milestones throughout the year, the leaders applied the new approach with their teams, who then provided feedback on what worked and what didn't. The top team's role-modeling sent a powerful signal to the broader organization, so much so that stories quickly spread as to how things were already changing down the line, even though the new system hadn't been formally rolled out.

The second pilot was run in HR, the thinking being that the HR team would need to provide support for the full roll-out and therefore needed to be upskilled in advance. Finally, scaled-down pilots of various parts of the process were conducted in a shortlist of locations and businesses to refine them and ensure they would translate into various cultural contexts.

> **Act**
> How do we manage the journey?

Test, learn, and scale: Pilot approach in controlled setting, distil learnings, adjust approach, and scale

Business-led governance: Ensure implementation is seen as business-led and overseen by a body with clear decision rights

Communication: Ensure expectations are clear, processes are transparent, and feedback can be given

5. Advance

AFTER EACH pilot, HR surveyed both managers and direct reports to assess the results and capture learnings and, more longitudinally, the Finance department kept a close eye on performance trends. The CEO reached out informally to key leaders for first-hand feedback and shared his personal excitement in leadership summits and other high-visibility events. At the end of the pilot period, the new approach, with some refinement, was deemed a win for both employees and for the bottom line of the business and so it was rolled out to the entire organization for the next full performance cycle, with the HR function acting as coaches. Throughout the rollout, pulse checks were used to gauge implementation success. Simultaneously, care was taken to embed the desired new skills and mindsets into all people processes, e.g. hiring interviews, CV scanning, and other recruiting initiatives, onboarding, and training. Importantly, part of the design was that the evaluations of managers explicitly took into account how well they managed performance in their teams, and how well they coached their leaders to do the same.

Advance
How do we keep moving forward?

Monitor impact: Keep close tabs on changes in performance and what can and can't be attributed to the new process

Ensure engagement: Regularly gauge managers' and employees' experience with running the new system

Institutionalize: Link to all aspects of performance culture including recruiting, onboarding, and talent management

TWO YEARS AFTER the initial employee survey that set the changes in motion, the senior team was delighted to see survey results indicated that motivation scores were on the rise across the board and that performance management in particular had gone from a performance demotivator for employees to a pride point, and one that helped them deliver more, better, and faster business results. A particularly positive, and somewhat unexpected finding, was that the shift from everyone being rated the same on a 5-point scale to ensuring real differentiation happened across a 3-point scale was seen as a great step forward by all but very few. Even those who ended up with lower ratings by and large indicated that they preferred knowing where they really stood and having an honest conversation than getting no real input at all. Outside of survey measures, the team also noted that voluntary attrition ("regretted departures") was now at an all-time low and, most importantly, business performance was stronger than ever.

PERFORMANCE MANAGEMENT:
AT A GLANCE

WHY IS IT IMPORTANT?

- Done well, it delivers results.
- What most companies are doing isn't working.
- More is known about what works than ever before.

WHAT ARE THE BIG IDEAS?

- Harmonize company and employee motives.
- Solve for fair process.
- Put skills first, not systems and data.

HOW DO I MAKE IT HAPPEN?

- Follow a five-step process to put in place the right approach.

  Most commonly neglected action in each step:

  Aspire: Make explicit design choices on all dimensions.

  Assess: Understand strengths, weaknesses of current state.

  Architect: Include mindset and capability interventions.

  Act: Make business leaders accountable to implement.

  Advance: Judge process success by business outcomes.

4

How do I create a high-performing leadership team?

High-Performing Teams:
A TIMELESS TOPIC

THE ORIGINS OF TEAMWORK go back to the dawn of human existence. In a world of hostile predators, early humans quickly learned that if they worked together they were far more able to fulfil the primal needs of safety, food, and protecting young, than by working alone. As we evolved, our teamwork became more sophisticated—it wasn't just about having more people to throw rocks at formidable creatures, but about leveraging the diverse skills inherent in the group, be it intellect, imagination, physical abilities, or other natural talents.

In the modern era the 1+1=3 nature of people working together can be seen across all aspects of our lives. In sports, the likes of France's 1998 football (soccer to some) World Cup championship team (unbeaten in the tournament, outscored opponents 15-2, and shut out Brazil in the title, equaling the most one-sided final ever), and the 1992 American men's basketball Olympic "Dream Team" (that won every game by an average of 44 points on its way to gold) showed how high-performing teams of talented athletes dominate the competition.

In music, the likes of Rodgers and Hammerstein (writers of musicals such as *The Sound of Music, South Pacific*, and *The King and I*, and winners of a staggering thirty-four Tony awards) and 1960s English rock band the Beatles (the best-selling band in history, having sold over 600 million units worldwide, and whose group magic and impact were never surpassed by its members' solo efforts) have shown the profound creativity that great teamwork can produce. In science it's not just talent, but great teamwork that put people on the moon and put an end to World War II. Even in the comic book world, the virtue of teamwork, is extolled with the likes of the Justice League, Avengers, and Fantastic Four.

In business the same is true, of course. Be it Henry Ford, Clarence Avery, Peter Martin, and Charles Sorenson (who together devised the assembly line in an effort to drive efficiency and reliability into all aspects of auto production), Walt Disney, Ub Iwerks, Roy Disney, and nine animators known as the "Nine Old Men" (who created some of the most memorable and profitable characters' in cartoon history, such as Mickey Mouse, Cinderella, and Snow White), or Google's Sergey Brin, Larry Page, Eric Schmidt, and Omid Kordestani (who created the most popular site on the Web)—a high-performing team at the top can have impact of industry- and history-shaping proportions.

In the spirit of these great accomplishments, we define a high-performing team as one that achieves superior results by working together in the pursuit of a common goal in ways that fully leverage the complementary talents and skills of its members. Henry Ford, known for his pithy and insightful one-liners, sums up the sentiment in saying, "Coming together is a beginning; keeping together is progress; working together is success."[1] Is your team a high-performing team? Read on to find out how to know for sure...and how to make sure!

TEAM OF ALL STARS

ALL STAR TEAM

High-performing teams achieve superior results by sharing a common goal and fully leveraging complementary talents

Why is it important?

TEAMWORK **BEATS TALENT** (BUT BOTH IS BEST)

THE 1992 ROSTER of the U.S. men's Olympic basketball team reads like a list of the greatest players in the history of the sport: Charles Barkley, Larry Bird, Patrick Ewing, Magic Johnson, Michael Jordan, Karl Malone, Scottie Pippen, and so on. Just bringing together the best players in the world wasn't enough to guarantee success, however. During their first month of practice in June of 1992, the dream team lost to a group of college players by eight points in a scrimmage. In the words of Michael Jordan, "We got killed today...we're so out of sync...we don't have any continuity at all."[2] Scottie Pippen put it more starkly, "We didn't know how to play with each other."[3] The loss woke the players up to the fact that winning was far more than being a team of all stars—it also required they be an all-star team. They adjusted accordingly, and the rest is history. As we've already mentioned, the "Dream Team" as they were referred to, dominated the competition—scoring over 100 points in every game and easily taking home the gold.

A more recent example of the power of teamwork over talent is that of the 2016 German National football (soccer to our American readers) team's World Cup win—becoming the first ever European team to do so in a competition held in the Americas. As per commentary from Søren Frank on World Soccer Talk, "The German victory was a result of team effort and a collective approach. In a way, no German player is a star. In another way, they are all stars.

Eleven (Germans) showed that they were more than Messi plus ten (Argentinians)...The German team has been set up by Löw [the coach] to function as a team, to work like a team, to defend like a team, and to attack like a team."[4]

In business the same is true. It's why savvy investors in start-ups often value the quality of the team and the quality of the interaction among the founding members more than the idea itself.[5] It's also why the quality of the management team is the single most important non-financial factor with 90 percent of investors when evaluating a new IPO.[6] It's also why there is a 1.9 times increased likelihood of having above-median financial performance when the top team is aligned and working together towards a common vision.[7] Social psychology further backs up the premise that teams beat individual talent in areas important to business success. For example, the American Psychological Association (APA) reports, "Groups of three or more perform better on complex problem-solving than the best of the same number of individuals."[8]

Reid Hoffman, LinkedIn co-founder, sums it up in saying, "No matter how brilliant your mind or strategy, if you're playing a solo game, you'll always lose out to a team."[9] Michael Jordan slam dunks the point with, "Talent wins games, but teamwork and intelligence win championships."[10]

90% of investors consider the top team as the most important non-financial factor when deciding to invest

1.9 / 1 likelihood of having above-median financial performance when top teams aligned and working together towards a common vision

"Talent wins games, but teamwork and intelligence win championships."
– Michael Jordan

The impact of team effectiveness on performance

Why is it important?
VERY **FEW** TEAMS
ACHIEVE GREATNESS

MAKE NO MISTAKE, great team work is hard work—especially at a senior level. Why? On one hand, such teams are filled with driven and opinionated leaders representing different perspectives, be they functions, products, lines of business, or geographies. They are all vying for influence and the allocation of constrained resources. Many are often also competing with one another for the next promotion, requiring them to assert unique perspectives and differentiate their performance from others. Accordingly, team members are typically watching their backs and maneuvering behind closed doors, even though in meetings they present a congenial and "here for the team" face.

As if these weren't challenging enough conditions, group dynamics gurus such as Dr. Kenwyn Smith and Dr. David Berg point out that group work is full of natural, unavoidable, and unsolvable paradoxes. The classic illustration of a paradox is as follows: "This next statement is true" and "The previous statement is false." Both statements are perfectly accurate, yet together they create a self-referential contradiction. In group life, paradoxes are everywhere: there is pressure to conform to the group, yet the power of the group comes from leveraging the individuality of its members (the identity paradox); motivation to be involved in the group is proportional to the ability to be removed (the involvement paradox); the work of those in power positions is to create the conditions in which others are powerful (the authority paradox); and so on.[11]

It's no wonder that only 6 percent of top HR executives report that "the executives in their C-suite are a well-integrated team".[12] Moreover, only 38 percent of executives agree that their top team has the right strategy, 35 percent that it effectively capitalizes on synergies, and 28 percent that they know their collective gaps and have a plan to address them.[13] What's more, top teams themselves report that they are less than 60 percent as effective as they would be if they worked better together. The team's leaders, however, often aren't fully in touch with this reality—on average they believe their teams are working at roughly 80 percent of their full potential.[14]

Raise your hand if you've ever been in a team where agreement is hard to reach. Or where leaders failed to act in concert and contradictory messages were sent to staff after a decision was made. Or where the team insularly blamed others for poor performance ("If only 'they' got it"—typically referring to lower levels). Or where either tough issues were avoided in the interest of maintaining harmonious relationships or dealing with them devolved into personal attacks. Or where team time was spent in status updates with little time for debate, and therefore seen largely as a waste of time. We think we're safe in assuming all of our readers will have a hand raised at this point.

Management thinker Richard Hackman once said, "I have no question that teams can create magic. I just don't count on it." As a leader, you shouldn't either.

SCALE OF 1 TO 7, 7 HIGHEST — UNTAPPED POTENTIAL

Team is effective overall	4.0
Decision-making processes clear	3.9
Deals with conflict	3.7
Puts company before BU interests	4.2
CEO provides effective direction	4.2

On average, CEOs rate their team 1.5 points higher on all dimensions

Perceptions of top team members of their team's performance

"I have no question that teams can create magic. I just don't count on it."
– Harvard Professor Richard Hackman, co-author of Senior Leadership Teams

Why is this important?
THE FUTURE WILL BE **MORE DEMANDING** OF TOP TEAMS

THERE'S LITTLE DEBATE that in business over the last fifty years, leadership has evolved from more hierarchical and dictatorial forms of control to more collaborative and empowering forms. This, in turn, has led to a rise in the importance of having teamwork at the top in order to facilitate the whole of a company performing better than the sum of its parts. But what does the future hold, and how will the demands on top teams change as a result?

When we look into our crystal ball we see that the digital age will radically reshape the notion of what the workplace is and how work gets done. Traditional offices may become obsolete, with work being done remotely as collaboration is enabled using virtual means. Accordingly, the war for talent will be waged on a truly global scale. Traditional company boundaries will be more porous: freelance talent will come and go and the number of partnerships will skyrocket, some extending as far as including customers and even competitors to solve problems and open up new growth opportunities. Technology will solve a number of operational issues, yet as automation and algorithms become commoditized and information more difficult to secure, human wisdom, judgement, and creativity will be the most powerful differentiators. The importance of the human factor will be further reinforced by moral, ethical, and environmental issues becoming requirements for winning in the marketplace.

Operating in this context, senior teams will undoubtedly have to up their game if they want their companies to be on top. They'll need to quickly and seamlessly assimilate and exit members in ways that extract the full value of their unique skills and vantage points. They'll need to harness the collective wisdom of team members scattered from Beijing to Barcelona to Boston. They'll need to solve problems with a systems perspective to maximize value in an open, dynamic environment.

CEOs are already feeling the pressure: 59 percent report that they face more threats to company growth than in the previous three years; 56 percent think that it is likely they will compete in new industries over the next three years and 51 percent will enter into new alliances or joint ventures in the next twelve months.[15] Against this backdrop, Steve Tappin interviewed over 150 CEOs in the research for his book, *The Secrets of CEOs*, and found, "Probably two-thirds of CEOs are struggling...Being a CEO has always been tough, but the global nature of modern business means running a company has become increasingly complex...About 90 percent struggle with work–life balance, when they talk off the record...The only way forward now is for much more of a team...A really tight team on a mission to create a brilliant company."[16]

Leadership expert John Maxwell once said, "Teamwork makes the dream work, but vision becomes a nightmare when the leader has a big dream and a bad team."[17] Make no mistake, these words will ring even truer tomorrow than today. We now turn to what the big ideas are to make the dream work.

% OF SENIOR EXECUTIVES WHO AGREE THEIR TOP TEAM/COMPANY:

Increasing challenges facing teams at the top

Faces more threats to company growth than in the previous three years **59%**

Is likely to compete in new industries over the next three years **56%**

Will face rising cross-sector competition **56%**

Will enter into new alliances or joint ventures in the next year **51%**

"The number of firms who consider effectiveness of management teams to be a major challenge rose from 58 percent in 2015 to 63 percent this year [2016]"
– *HR* magazine

"Two thirds of CEOs are struggling ...the only way forward now is for much more of a team"
– Steve Tappin,
The Secrets of CEOs

What are the big ideas?
DRIVE AND MEASURE PROGRESS ON **THREE DIMENSIONS**

MUCH HAS BEEN WRITTEN about high-performing teams, yet how much do leaders really remember and use? Most of our readers will have seen Patrick Lencioni's work on the *Five Dysfunctions of a Team*—can you cite them? And what to do to overcome them? How about former McKinsey partner John Katzenbach's *The Wisdom of Teams*—do you recall what makes the difference between a working group and a high-performing team?

In our experience, leaders are best served thinking about teams in terms of a simple and highly intuitive framework that involves just three dimensions, which are best and most memorably discovered drawing on one's own experience. The first step is to think about your work in teams over your career; what would you describe as a "peak experience"—the team environment in which you were able to perform at your personal best? Now, with that in mind, think about words that describe that environment: what was it that enabled you to be at your peak? We've conducted this exercise with more than 5,000 executives during workshops over the last decade, and the results are remarkably consistent.

One set of words can be grouped in the category alignment on direction, for example: "clear goal," "milestones," "access to resources," and "sponsorship." A second set falls into the category quality of interaction: "constructive conflict," "good communication," "trust," the "right skills," and "diversity of views." The final set, including "meaningful," "learning," "against the odds," and "never done before" relate to a strong sense of renewal. This exercise reveals the three essential dimensions of teamwork:

ALIGNMENT: Shared goals and assumptions about the business and shared beliefs about the purpose of the team in relation to achieving those goals.

INTERACTION: The right mix of skills and perspectives brought to bear in an environment characterized by high trust, open communication, and constructive conflict (for those readers familiar with Google's "Project Aristotle," these are the norms that create psychological safety).[18]

RENEWAL: An environment where calculated risks can be taken, outside ideas listened to and learned from, and where achieving the outcome is deeply meaningful—the work being done matters.

The exercise gets particularly potent when we ask leaders how much more productive they were when working in this environment than in the "average" working environment. The responses center around five times more productive—a number our research and experience confirm. How often are these conditions in place when your top team works together? If you don't know you should ask— and then take steps to get more. The math is clear: if your team gets into this zone even a relatively modest twenty additional percentage points more of the time, its members will be five times more productive, and the productivity of your team's work together will almost double!

ALIGNMENT	INTERACTION	RENEWAL
Do we have a shared view and commitment on where and how to lead the organization?	Do we have high-quality interactions that drive superior decisions and execution?	Are we energized to lead, learn from others, and shape our external environment?

Three dimensions of top team performance: Alignment on direction, quality of interaction, and sense of renewal

"Interaction, alignment, and renewal are all interdependent. Teams need to go forward simultaneously on all three fronts to make progress."
McKinsey Quarterly

What are the big ideas?
FOCUS THE TEAM ON DOING THE **WORK ONLY IT CAN DO**

ONE OF the most common complaints voiced by members of low-performing teams is "we spend too much time in meetings." The well-intentioned response from leaders is typically to adjust the team's operating rhythm, consolidating meetings and reducing the related travel burden. Yet somehow, much to the leader's dismay, this only exacerbates the problem. The reason is that the real issue is less about the absolute amount of time spent, and more about how the time is spent. The above-mentioned changes simply mean more is packed into less time in a less effective format, making the time spent feel even more senseless compared to attending to what individual team members perceive as the "real work" of driving results in the areas they lead. This is proved by the numbers: only 38 percent of CEO direct reports feel their top team is focused on work that truly benefits from a top-team perspective and only 35 percent feel the right amount of time is allocated to important topics.

So what should senior teams focus on? Of course the specifics depend on the context, strategy, and composition of any given team, but there are certain topics no other group is better suited to work on. Among these are: corporate strategy (priorities, targets, M&A); large-scale allocation of resources; identifying synergies and interdependencies across business units; validating decisions that significantly affect all employees; assuring delivery of company financial targets; providing direction for major company-wide projects; reinforcing the desired company culture (including individual and collective role modeling), and building the company's leadership bench strength (which includes providing feedback to one another). What teams should not focus on are any topics that can be done better in individual functions or lines of business.

Equally important as the topics on the agenda are the norms by which they are discussed. In our experience, high-performing teams ensure that any informational items are covered outside of the meeting format and that for topics covered live at least 80 percent of the time is spent in discussion vs. listening to presentations. Other powerful norms include: holding each other to a "no-blame" standard (there is nothing in the company the senior team shouldn't take responsibility for); putting company needs ahead of business unit/function needs; showing cabinet solidarity outside of the room and making sure there is ample "team-only" time (without guest presenters) so that there is sufficient time for otherwise confidential views to be shared, and so on. These kind of norms can easily become just "words on a page" if the leader, or someone on the team, isn't skilled in ensuring that meetings run in a manner where both the "what" and "how" work in concert.

A senior leader wouldn't ask members of her or his team to schedule their own meetings or book their own travel—these activities can be done better and more cost-effectively by others. Leaders are wise to apply the same logic to how their top team spends their time together, keeping it focused on only those areas where it adds the most value.

Only 38% of top team members believe their teams focus on value-adding topics

Only 35% of top team members believe their teams spend the right amount of time on relevant topics

DO TOGETHER
- Strategy and tradeoffs
- Enterprise resource allocation
- Synergies across business units
- Top 200 talent decisions
- External engagement

TAKE IT OUTSIDE
- Business unit-level strategy, capital allocations, performance reviews, and talent decisions
- Detailed initiative planning and reporting
- Informational topics

The challenge of working on the right things, and what to do about it

What are the big ideas?

DON'T LET STRUCTURE DICTATE WHO IS ON THE TEAM

HOW MANY PLAYERS are there on a World Cup soccer team? Most people would say eleven, but there are actually twenty-three registered on each squad. How many on an Olympic volleyball team? Many would say six, but the answer is twelve. Who is on the top team of your company? Harvard professor Ruth Wagerman and her colleagues asked members of more than 120 top teams around the world this question and found that fewer than 10 percent agreed. In those cases where there was agreement, there was a high correlation with the team being considered a high-performing team.[19]

This, of course, begs the question of who should be on the leadership team? To answer this, leaders should heed the research that says more than ten diminishes effectiveness. As the size grows beyond this, the dynamics tend to result in sub-teams forming, less individual ownership is taken for group objectives, and the sheer amount of time required for everyone to participate is unmanageable (not only creating less robust debate, but increasing the likelihood of group-think taking over as an unconscious means of speeding up the process). On the flipside, leaders should beware of creating teams of less than six. Below this the lack of diversity in perspectives lowers the quality of decision-making, the bandwidth of sponsorship for company-wide initiatives becomes a bottleneck, and succession-planning issues become more acute (both in the form of a limited pool, and excessive competition and related politics).

By bounding the size of the team to between six and ten, many CEOs will face a predicament—they now can't have all their direct reports at the table. Precisely. We believe there should be no assumption that "job title is membership" on a top team. Instead, leaders should configure it based on the precise knowledge, capabilities, experience, diverse views, and attitude needed to do the work that only the top team can do. This line of thinking isn't comfortable for many CEOs because it means they can't be overly inclusive, held hostage by star performers who aren't team players, or avoid emotionally tough conversations (removing members, for example). For some CEOs this means moving to a model of multiple teams: an operating committee to handle near-term performance issues, a strategy committee to drive longer-term growth and innovation issues, and a people committee to handle team and talent-related issues. Some leaders are involved in all of them, while others may only be on one.

Once the configuration of the team (or teams) is set, a leader is wise to let a team season before judging their collective performance. Research is clear that newness is a liability to effectiveness (consider studies of commercial airline pilots that find 73 percent of the incidents in its database occur on a crew's first day flying together before they've learned to work as a team).[20] The seasoning process can be accelerated via a "field and forum" journey combining facilitated workshops engaged in the real work of the team (not the "trust fall"-type exercises too often used in team-building activities!) with structured cycles of action and reflection built in between sessions—which takes us to the "how" of creating a high-performing leadership team.

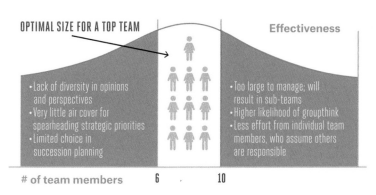

OPTIMAL SIZE FOR A TOP TEAM

Effectiveness

- Lack of diversity in opinions and perspectives
- Very little air cover for spearheading strategic priorities
- Limited choice in succession planning

- Too large to manage; will result in sub-teams
- Higher likelihood of groupthink
- Less effort from individual team members, who assume others are responsible

# of team members   6   10

The optimal size of a top team and why

"Having a huge senior leadership team—say, one that includes all of the CEO's direct reports—may be worse than having no team at all."
– Harvard Professor Richard Hackman, co-author of *Senior Leadership Teams*

How do I make it happen?
FOLLOW A **FIVE-STEP PROCESS** TO BUILD YOUR TEAM

CONFRONTED WITH STAGNATING prices and rising competition from Asia, a Latin American metals and mining company shifted to a more integrated strategy. As part of this, the structure was evolved from a series of independent business units to a fully matrixed organization. The highly ambitious and successful CEO realized that in order for this new strategy and structure to work, he would need a different dynamic at the top. In the past, his Executive Committee meetings were largely information-sharing events; his top team members focused relentlessly on delivering their own unit's performance without much thought for the group as a whole. Going forward, his ExCo would need to become a real team that genuinely optimized performance and made trade-offs across the group.

1. Aspire

THE CEO BEGAN by reviewing the composition of his team, considering where each of the top thirty leaders would sit on a "skill/will" matrix. On one axis were the skills he felt would be important to have on the team for success in the future. This included "hard" skills such as business acumen, analytic problem-solving capability, and technical competence in their role. It also included "soft" skills such as leading change, emotional intelligence, and relationship building. On the other axis, the "will" axis, he considered factors such as the extent to which they saw the challenges and opportunities for the company in the same way he did, the sense of ownership and accountability they felt for the enterprise to be successful, their desire to role-model a new culture, and the grit and energy they had to persevere through obstacles.

The exercise was enlightening in many respects. On one hand, he hadn't fully internalized the importance of moving some clear blockers off the team. Two of his direct reports would have to go. Second, four leaders from one level below his team were high potentials and he needed to find a way to increase their profile and responsibility. Third, he saw a clear gap in the ability to lead transformational change at scale in operations, and for this role he'd need to look outside the company. He moved quickly to put as much of his new, hand-picked ExCo in place. He asked his head of HR to plan for a team effectiveness offsite as soon as the majority were on board.

Aspire
Where do we want to go?

Strategic imperative: Identify the competencies and technical skills the team will need to deliver on your strategy

Team mandate: Clarify the cut-off between top-team and business-unit remits

Complementarity: Map team members to determine whether they have complementary, skills, experience, thinking styles, and networks

Team parameters: Decide on who is formally considered as part of the team

2. Assess

WHEN THE TEAM got together six weeks later, most members were expecting a lot of talk about personality types and the sort of team-building exercises, such as rope courses or constructing bikes together, that they had experienced in the past. Instead, they were surprised to engage in intense, rigorous conversations on the role the team would play—both as a whole and as individuals—in delivering against the business strategy. HR had set the session up for success, having spoken to each of the members in advance and conducted a pre-survey, so hard data was available to focus discussion on the areas that mattered most.

The first order of business was to ensure there was alignment on the new strategy. It turned out that everyone could recite the same words, but when asked what the top five priorities were for the enterprise to deliver the strategy it was enlightening to find that the team of eight had individually mentioned over thirty priorities (if they were fully aligned, they would all have mentioned the same five!). Next, they worked together on what it would take to execute against the priorities, and what was the role of the team in unlocking performance. This session gave a fuller appreciation to each individual of why the members of the team were who they were, and clarity was given on what would—and what wouldn't—be part of the team's mandate.

In advance of the offsite, the HR team had also mapped each individual's professional networks against the key stakeholders (internal and external) required to deliver against the business strategy. Sharing this data led to a robust discussion and clear assignments of who would cover who in the needed network. The team then had a candid conversation about the mindsets and behaviors which could block the delivery of all they had agreed, and committed to a set of norms.

Assess
How ready are we to go there?

Team baseline: Assemble a robust fact base on how effective your top team is in terms of alignment, interaction, and renewal

Network reach: Determine the collective breadth and depth of the team's networks

Mindsets: Understand what mindset shifts would enable the team to unlock higher organizational performance

Common language: Agree what high performance means in terms of the team's purpose, priorities, norms, etc.

3. Architect

COMING OUT OF THE SESSION, the CEO was pleased with where the team had got to but knew one offsite wasn't going to be enough. In discussions with HR and experts in team effectiveness, an overall journey was crafted. Key elements would be quarterly, professionally facilitated offsites that would contain both action sessions (doing the real work of the business) and reflection sessions (reflecting on how the work was getting done, and determining how to improve). Time would also be put aside over meals to get to know each other more deeply as people to strengthen the trust base in the team. Monthly in-person business review meetings would be observed by a team effectiveness expert whose role would be the team "conscience" to ensure the team lived up to the commitments they'd made.

A decision was also made to provide two members with one-on-one coaching, as it became clear during the working session that they were lagging the group in their vision of what was expected—and possible—for both the company and team. Finally, a number of new opportunities for individuals to work together were set up. This included creating some "unlikely pairings" of team members as sponsors of corporate initiatives (vs. having individual sponsors), making town halls ExCo vs. CEO-only events, and featuring a broad range of ExCo members in corporate communications on enterprise topics.

Architect
What do we need to do to get there?

Field-and-forum design: Decide on the number, frequency, and structure of the sessions for the leadership team

Quick wins: Build small wins and symbolic actions into existing interactions to allow team to experience new ways of working together

Coaching methods: Decide on type, frequency, and duration of group and individual coaching sessions (if needed)

4. Act

THE MONTHLY TEAM coaching and quarterly working sessions went forward as planned, and having an external facilitator for the latter was valued by all members as it enabled everyone to be fully engaged in the work and to feel confident closure would be reached on topics in reasonable timeframes. One of the sessions that took the team by surprise was a dinner conversation where everyone was asked to share a memorable story from their childhood.

After initial eye-rolling at what seemed to be a very "soft" exercise, they ended up sharing stories until the early hours of the morning, deepening connections in ways they hadn't experienced before, in spite of many having known each other for a long time. The next day they agreed "it was the best conversation we've had in years."

At the second quarterly offsite, a substantive "reflection" session was held on how the team was working together, informed by a survey of the individual members and their reports. The good news was that the team was being perceived as "one team" more than ever. It was also clear, however, that irritation was being built up. The facilitator didn't let them sidestep the causes—if these weren't dealt with, they'd become major problems. The heart of the issue was that doing what was best for the group, even if it meant "losing" in one's unit, proved easier said than done, and the new matrix structure with its more diluted decision rights added to the tensions. Once surfaced, the issues were tackled head-on through "field work"—a facilitated process of using real work that needed to be done as the crucible to working through solutions.

Act
How do we manage the journey?

Team forum sessions: Practice new ways of working by doing real work in facilitated sessions on topics requiring top-team ownership

Fieldwork assignments: Identify enterprise-wide business opportunities where the top team can practice ways of working together and add real value

360-degree feedback: Interweave individual and team development by using 360-degree feedback and ensuring each team member shares what they have learned with others

5. Advance

OVER TIME the team adopted a number of working norms that helped them self-regulate. One was a "yellow card," printed with the agreed-upon norms. Everyone carried one, and it was pulled out and held up as a way of calling "time out" when norms were being violated. At first the team worried that it would become annoying, but they soon saw the power of a symbol to trigger everyone to lift themselves out of the heat of the moment and reflect on what they had agreed in terms of how to work together. They also migrated to using an electronic polling system during discussions so that they could gauge the pulse of the room efficiently (in the words of one team member, "It lets us all speak at once") and avoid group-think. Also, a norm of having no more than three PowerPoint pages shared in the room (if necessary, more information could be shared as a pre-read) ensured the focus of time was on discussion, not presentation.

When issues such as unexpected losses in a business due to changes in the commodities market reared their head, the CEO made it a team issue, whereas in the past he would have handled it directly with the head of the business then divided up the shortfall and demanded it of the other businesses. In working through the issues together, more creative and effective solutions were found that often turned setbacks into catalysts for innovation.

Advance
How do we keep moving forward?

Alignment of support systems: Ensure supporting structure and processes for the top team are in place and working well

Ongoing coaching and monitoring: Continue to monitor effectiveness against desired goals and baseline, introducing occasional coaching events to sustain a sense of renewal

Succession planning: Routinely scan for the next generation of leaders and ensure they are well versed in the role and behavioral norms of the top team

AT THE END of the first year of the journey, formal stock was again taken on effectiveness as viewed by the team itself as well as those beneath them. Alignment, interaction, and renewal scores were high—fueled by the fact that the company's strategy was paying dividends. Everyone was particularly proud and grateful that the question, "I trust my other team members" received an average score of 10 out of 10. In spite of the positive result, the team set its sights on how they could be even better in the coming year. Informed by individual 360 feedback data, as well as the team feedback, they revised the role statement, norms, and upped their commitment to working together as a high-performing team.

HIGH-PERFORMING TEAMS:
AT A GLANCE

 WHY IS IT IMPORTANT?

- Teamwork beats talent (but both is best).
- Very few teams achieve greatness.
- The future will be more demanding of top teams.

 WHAT ARE THE BIG IDEAS?

- Drive and measure progress on three dimensions.
- Focus the team on doing the work only it can do.
- Don't let structure dictate who is on the team.

 HOW DO I MAKE IT HAPPEN?

- Follow a five-step process to build your team.

  Most commonly neglected action in each step:

  Aspire: Agree on a clear definition and measures of success.

  Assess: Solve for complementary skills, experience, thinking.

  Architect: Design a clear field and forum journey.

  Act: Leverage periodic individual and team 360s.

  Advance: Thoughtfully prepare and expose the next generation.

II. DECISION -MAKING AND DESIGN

Chapter **5**

How do I improve the quality and speed of decision-making?

We acknowledge McKinsey Senior Partner Aaron DeSmet
for his work in co-authoring this chapter.

Decision-Making:
A TIMELESS TOPIC

"ONE DAY Alice came to a fork in the road and saw a Cheshire cat in a tree. 'Which road do I take?' she asked. 'That depends a good deal on where you want to get to,' was his response. 'I don't much care where—', Alice answered. 'Then,' said the cat, 'it doesn't matter which way you walk.'"

This famous decision-making advice comes from English mathematician Charles Lutwidge Dodgson, better known as his pseudonym, Lewis Carroll, in his classic children's tale *Alice's Adventures in Wonderland*, penned in 1865. Go back in time and you'll find real-world versions of the Cheshire cat giving decision-making guidance to Alice: the iChing in China (using seemingly random numbers to determine divine intent); the Oracle of Delphi in Greece (through which the god Apollo was believed to speak), and, in other cultures, entrails, smoke, dreams, and the like have all been used to guide decisions.[1]

If you look around today for decision-making advice, prepare to be overwhelmed. You'll find many rational models that assume there is one best, optimal outcome (e.g. SWOT, Pareto, Decision trees, Pugh matrix), bounded rational models that recognize it's not possible to consider all possible outcomes, predictably irrational models (e.g. Chip and Dan Heath's WRAP model) and many decision-making process models (autocratic, consultative, group, etc.). There are so many models, in fact, that there are now decision-making models for deciding which one to use!

The preoccupation and proliferation of advice related to decision-making makes sense when one considers that an adult makes about 35,000 at least somewhat conscious decisions each day.[2] The vast majority of these are relatively easy and inconsequential (e.g. whether to button the shirt from the top or the bottom), yet others require more thought and have more significant cumulative impact (e.g. how to prioritize one's time), and still others can be life-altering in and of themselves (e.g. a career path to pursue).

Turning from individual to organizational life, in an organization of 50,000 employees (the rough average of the Fortune 500) we estimate there are over 400 million decisions made per day. In the spirit of Albert Camus' famous assertion, that life is the "sum of all your choices," we argue that in organizational life "success is the sum of all decisions."[3] Like individual decisions, these may be small but, cumulatively, highly consequential, such as the choices your frontline makes in interacting with your customers, or big and substantive decisions in and of themselves such as capital investments—where, when, and how to go to market—or decisions to expand or shut down an operation.

Are there ways to improve the quality and speed of decision-making in your organization as it relates to achieving your business objectives? Read on to decide.

...THERE ARE **400 MILLION** DECISIONS MADE PER DAY

SUCCESS IS THE SUM OF ALL DECISIONS

Decision-making is the process by which a choice is selected from available options

Why is it important?

DECISION QUALITY CAN MAKE OR BREAK A COMPANY

IT'S 1975. You are a senior leader at one of the world's most successful and iconic companies. You and your 120,000 employees dominate the mass-market consumer photography industry. Your model is perfect—you sell the camera (for which you have an 85 percent share of the U.S. market) and then people return again and again to buy your film to record the important events in their lives (you have a 95 percent share of the film market). In addition, you have a huge business processing film into pictures to put into photo albums. Your value proposition is summed up in your tagline, "You press the button, we do the rest."

You're sitting in a presentation by a 24-year-old electrical engineer, Steve Sassan, titled "Filmless photography." As it turns out, you're witnessing the unveiling of the world's first prototype megapixel digital camera, and you're on point to decide what to do with Steve's invention. As he presents, you are reminded of the proud history of innovation in the company—a company that literally invented the roll of film, and recently pioneered the instant camera space. Yet filmless photography? Who wants to see a picture on a TV screen? More importantly, what would this do to your current business model—to put this on the market would kill the golden goose! Decision time, and all eyes turn to you ...and you hear yourself declare the business equivalent of, "It's cute, but don't tell anyone about it."[4] Bad decision.

As many readers will have already surmised, this is the true story of what happened at Eastman Kodak. Having invented the digital camera, they buried it so their film-based business model was not disrupted. As a result, the company fell behind in the digital era and never caught up. In 2012, when social media had made button-pressing more popular than ever before (see Facebook, Flickr, Instagram, etc.), Kodak filed for bankruptcy. Today it has 6,500 employees.

Eastman Kodak is by no means alone in making bad decisions regarding industry disruptions. IBM invented the personal computer, but couldn't imagine a future away from mainframes and the company had to be reinvented under a different CEO and management team. Motorola invented digital phones, but didn't want to step away from the pagers and analog phone business that made up the bulk of their profits and fell behind the competition.

On the flip side, where would Intel be without the decision to aggressively brand its otherwise anonymous ingredient inside a computer as "Intel Inside"? Where would Boeing be had it not made the bold decision to invest more than Boeing's net worth in the 707, which ended up remaking the company, industry, and culture of its time? What would IBM have become had Lou Gerstner not put the brakes on the plan to break up the company that were underway when he took over? These were good decisions, and ones that literally "made" the companies in question.

The Harvard Business Review sums it up well in declaring, "Any one decision could be the first decision down the path to corporate collapse."[5] ...Or greatness, we'd add.

EXAMPLES OF GOOD DECISIONS	EXAMPLES OF BAD DECISIONS	
Intel branding "Intel Inside"	**AOL's** decision to merge with Time Warner	*Examples of good and bad business decisions*
Boeing betting the company on the 707	**Kodak's** decision not to pursue the digital camera	

"Making good decisions is a crucial skill at every level...it needs to be taught explicitly to everyone in organizations." – Peter Drucker, management thinker

Why is it important?
POOR DECISION-MAKING IS RAMPANT

THE HARVEY FAMILY is sitting around a porch in Coleman, Texas. It's 104 degrees out, but the porch is shaded, so everyone is reasonably comfortable. Jerry Harvey's father-in-law says, "Hey, why don't we drive to Abilene and have dinner at the cafeteria." Jerry thinks to himself, "This is crazy; I don't want to drive fifty-three miles in the heat of summer in a 1958 Buick to have dinner in a lousy cafeteria." Before he can speak up, his wife interjects, "Sure, that sounds like a good idea." Jerry then hedges, "OK, I guess…assuming your mother wants to go." Jerry's mother-in-law affirms, "Of course I want to go."

Four hours and 106 miles later they return to the porch, covered in sweat and dust from driving in the brutal heat with the windows down (there is no air conditioning in a 1958 Buick!). The food, as per Jerry's prediction, had been almost unpalatable. As they sit down, Jerry says sarcastically, "Well, that was a great trip, wasn't it?" Nobody speaks. His mother-in-law then finally says, "To tell the truth, I didn't enjoy it. I'd have rather stayed home, but you all pressured me into going." Jerry responds, "I didn't pressure you, I was happy here, I only went to make the rest of you happy." His wife then says, "But I was just going to make you all happy." Jerry's father-in-law then speaks up, "I never wanted to go to Abilene, I just thought you all might be bored sitting at home!"

We've borrowed this story from Dr. Jerry B. Harvey's 1974 landmark book on organizational behavior, *The Abilene Paradox, and Other Meditations on Management*, as it's a wonderful illustration of how absurd group decision-making can become (in this case in the form of what is commonly referred to as "Group Think"). But surely this kind of dysfunctional decision-making doesn't happen in today's large organizations, right? Think again. Most employees don't have to think for long to come up with examples of when a senior person has said, "I wonder if..." which then spawns a set of analyses, further research, and soon a project is born that takes on a life of its own that leads to nowhere.

Whether the result of dynamics related to the Abilene Paradox or other decision-making dysfunctions that may exist, the sad fact is that only 28 percent of employees feel the quality of strategic decisions in their companies is generally good.[6] The upside, of course, is that this means there is a significant opportunity for companies that focus on improving the quality and speed of decision-making. Research suggests such efforts can increase the speed of decision-making by 40–50 percent, create a 10–25 percent reduction in executive time spent in meetings, and 5–15 percent of general and administrative cost savings. Most importantly, the perceived quality of their decision-making increases by 35–40 percent.[7]

To put that into perspective, if the average adult increased the speed (which in this case can also be considered a proxy for quality) with which they run 100 meters by 35 percent, they'd be faster than Usain Bolt, the world's fastest man. World champion, record- setting, gold-medal-worthy decision-making in your reach!

AVERAGE IMPACT OF IMPROVEMENT EFFORTS

Only **28%** of employees feel the quality of their company's strategic decisions are generally good

40–50%	faster decisions
35–40%	higher quality decisions
30–40%	better execution of decisions
10–25%	reduction in meeting time
05–15%	general administrative cost savings

Improvement potential for decision-making

Why is it important?
IT AFFECTS YOUR
ABILITY TO RETAIN TALENT

IN OUR CAREERS as business consultants, we estimate that we have each sat in over 15,000 meetings in which decisions have been made. In some of these, we feel we've witnessed what we'd consider decision-making brilliance—game-changing calls full of insight and foresight. Others, however, have been decidedly less spectacular.

In spite of our best efforts as advisors, we've seen teams spend more time wrestling with the question of whether or not to serve breakfast at an offsite than they've spent on the substance of the offsite. We've seen decisions on acquisition targets go round in circles while competitors have swept up the targets in question. We've seen senior leaders make calls on frontline-level issues uninformed by relevant facts and without ever having set foot out of their corporate offices. In these cases, we have to be honest, one of the thoughts we have leaving the meetings is, "Phew, I'm so glad I don't work there!"

We're not alone in connecting decision-making with the desire to join and stay at a company. Look at virtually any study of employee retention and you'll see decision-making effectiveness and involvement are key drivers. One such study that looked across eighteen countries showed that "Satisfaction with the organization's business decisions" is the number one driver of retention in Switzerland, number two in the United States, and number four in China. More broadly, looking across all countries studied, the importance of a different kind of decision rises to the top—the number two driver of employee retention overall was found to be: "Satisfaction with the organization's people decisions." Looking through the lens of employee engagement tells a similar story about the importance of decision-making, but from a different angle: the number four driver of engagement globally is "input in decisions in my department," which ranks far ahead of other drivers such as "challenging work," "career advancement opportunities," and "good relationship with my supervisor."[8]

The story of Yahoo! is a cautionary tale. As they struggled to decide whether they were a tech or media company, they let Google, founded some four years after Yahoo!, surpass them by launching the likes of Gmail, Google+, the Android operating system, and Google Apps.[9] The cumulative impact of Yahoo!'s decision-making challenges on its talent retention have been well documented and were perhaps best summarized by the 2011 *Wall Street Journal* article, "Yahoo battles Brain Drain."[10]

At this point we hope you're decidedly in agreement with us that decision-making can make or break a company, is an area with improvement potential in most companies—and whether or not it's done well has major talent retention implications.

Enough with the "why," then, and on to the "what."

UNITED STATES

1. Have excellent career advancement opportunities
2. Satisfaction with the organization's business decisions
3. Good relationship with supervisor
4. Organization's reputation as a great place to work
5. Ability to balance my work/personal life

GLOBAL

1. Organization's reputation as a great place to work
2. Satisfaction with the organization's people decisions
3. Good relationship with supervisor
4. Understand potential career track within organization
5. Ability to balance my work/personal life

Where decision-making ranks as a driver of talent retention

What are the big ideas?

DIFFERENTIATE AMONG
THREE TYPES OF DECISIONS

ONE OF the most famous stories about decision-making effectiveness comes from C. Northcote Parkinson in his 1958 book, *The Pursuit of Progress.* As the story goes, a finance committee has to make three investment decisions. First, they discuss the investment of a £10 million nuclear power plant. This decision gets approved in 2.5 minutes. The next agenda item is to decide which color to paint their bike shed (total cost about £350). After a 45-minute discussion, the decision is made. Third, a new coffee machine needs to be acquired for the staff, which will roughly cost £21. The committee discusses this topic for 1 hour and 15 minutes and decides to postpone the decision to the next meeting. Parkinson calls this phenomenon the law of triviality (also known as the bike-shed effect), or the tendency for organizations to give disproportionate attention to trivial issues and details (a phenomenon, as we've mentioned earlier, that we've witnessed too often in board rooms!).[11]

The law of triviality is one of many dysfunctions that affect the speed and quality of decision-making. The first step in avoiding such dysfunction is to differentiate between three decision types:

TYPE A: INFREQUENT, HIGH-STAKES DECISIONS that affect the enterprise broadly (e.g. major mergers and acquisitions, investing in new technologies, hiring a new CEO). These decisions warrant disciplined decision-making processes that ensure the right data is gathered, open dialogue and debate take place, and all stakeholders' voices are involved and aligned to the greatest extent possible. These types of decisions happen with stage gates and include multiple techniques to avoid biases.

TYPE B: REPETITIVE DECISIONS THAT CAN BE DELEGATED (to an individual or natural working team, e.g. regional or country-level marketing promotions, adjustments to site-level manufacturing operations, and, yes, which color to paint the bike shed!). These decisions should be delegated to the lowest possible level with clear and transparent accountabilities, both for making the decision and whom to consult (those consulted don't have a "vote," just input). These decisions should also come with clear, delegated authority such that levels of materiality or risk trigger additional approvals.

TYPE C: REPETITIVE, CROSS-CUTTING DECISIONS (which affect multiple areas, e.g. budget allocations across products/regions, sales and operations planning, new product development). These decisions are not, in fact, one decision, but instead the culmination of a chain of smaller decisions which must be coordinated and aligned across organizational boundaries. As such, a formal process that clearly defines decision protocols, particular at key interfaces, should be put in place across the end-to-end system. These processes should also have in-built feedback loops to enable the process to be systematically improved over time.

Dan Ariely, professor of behavioral economics and author of *Predictably Irrational*, summarizes well when he says, "Good decisions take time and attention, and the only way we can find the needed time and attention is by choosing our spots."[12]

FREQUENCY/ FAMILIARITY

INVOLVEMENT/ IMPORTANCE		Infrequent/unfamiliar	Frequent/familiar
Broad/more important		**TYPE A** • Right data and involvement • Stage-gate • Apply multiple tools to de-bias	**TYPE C** • Formal process with clear roles • Shared language • Feedback loops
Narrow/less important		No formal process required	**TYPE B** • Delegate • Clear accountability and transparency • Risk thresholds

How to tailor your decision-making approach

What are the big ideas?

DIALOGUE IS AS (OR MORE) IMPORTANT THAN DATA

"IN GOD WE TRUST, all others bring data" is a famous quote often attributed to management scientist, W. Edwards Deming. The quote espoused his fundamental philosophy that data measurement and analysis are essential to making good management decisions. Most leaders in modern business accept this as common sense—get the right data, you'll make the right decision. Ironically, the data doesn't fully back up this assertion!

In a cross-industry study of 1,048 major decisions made over five years (e.g. including new product investments, M&A, capital expenditures), managers were asked to report on the quality and detail of the data analysis done (e.g. building a detailed financial model, doing sensitivity analysis) and robustness of dialogue (e.g. the right participants engaging in high quality of debate). This information, combined with performance metrics, was then analyzed to determine how much the variance in results was explained by dialogue vs. data. The answer: dialogue wins—by a factor of six![13] This doesn't mean data doesn't matter, but does mean high-quality analytics are relatively useless without a high-quality dialogue to interpret, evaluate, and draw out the implications from it.

While the above study was of type A decisions, our experience is dialogue is important across all decision-types that matter in an organization, though looks different for each. For type B decisions that are delegated to individuals or natural working teams, this is why it is vital not just to assign the accountability, but also to be clear on who needs to be consulted by that individual or group in advance of making the decision. What's more, when the need to escalate a decision is triggered, the process should involve "picking up the phone" and having a conversation vs. anything cumbersome or bureaucratic.

When it comes to type C decisions, dialogue is vital as it ensures that the needed points of alignment across organizational boundaries happen efficiently and effectively. Leaders at these interfaces play pivotal roles in decision-making as they need to balance advocacy and inquiry to influence the process to move forward, without having authority to dictate action. Leaders are wise to ensure the right skill sets are present in these roles. To facilitate dialogue, it's also important to make sure everyone knows their role—else the all-too-common "no one can say yes, but everyone can say no" scenario appears.

There are many models to help leaders assign "positions" in decision-making, one of the most popular being the RACI model. This model involves clarifying who is responsible for making a recommendation, who approves it and therefore makes the actual decision, who is consulted before it is made, and who is informed after the decision has been taken.

In spite of Deming's emphasis on data, we suspect he'd agree that dialogue is as (or more) important. After all, he also is noted for saying, "3 percent of the problems have figures, 97 percent of the problems do not."[14]

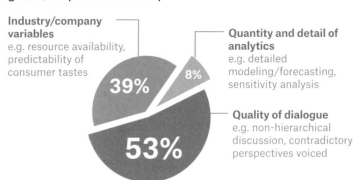

Industry/company variables
e.g. resource availability, predictability of consumer tastes
39%

Quantity and detail of analytics
e.g. detailed modeling/forecasting, sensitivity analysis
8%

Quality of dialogue
e.g. non-hierarchical discussion, contradictory perspectives voiced
53%

Drivers of whether a decision is good (creates desired performance improvement)

"Good process, in short, isn't just good hygiene; it's good business"
– McKinsey Quarterly

What are the big ideas?

WATCH OUT FOR **BIASES**

WE RETURN to the story of the Eastman Kodak Company that we discussed earlier in this chapter. By 2005, it was clear that the company's film revenues were nose-diving and the company would need to reinvent itself. Enter a new CEO, Antonio Perez. Perez quickly redirected the company's strategy towards what critics refer to as "intense, futile competition in the digital printer market."[15] So faulty was the strategy that under his leadership the price of Kodak shares decreased from around twenty-five dollars to less than one dollar by the end of 2011, leading to its filing for bankruptcy early the following year, earning Perez the dubious honor of being named one of the worst CEOs of 2011 by CNBC.

Why did Perez pursue a strategy that ran Kodak into the ground? The answer, at least in part, lies in what psychologists refer to as a confirmation bias. As he looked at the information available, he weighted information that confirmed his beliefs and ignored information refuting them (including that the company had already experimented in the space several times without success and lacked manufacturing expertise or scale to achieve attractive returns in such a commoditized industry).[16] His career before CEO? Twenty-five years working primarily in the inkjet printing and imaging areas of Hewlett-Packard.

The confirmation bias is just one of a multitude of cognitive biases (check Wikipedia and you'll find a list of over 120 listed) that cause our decisions to deviate from good judgement. In our experience, however, this and two others are the most prevalent and dangerous: the social bias and the optimism bias. Social bias is the tendency to overweight considerations regarding how favorably we believe others will view a decision. This is precisely what happens in the "Abilene Paradox" we described earlier. Optimism bias is the expectation that the best possible outcome will emerge. This accounts for why divorce rates in the western world are around 40 percent, yet when you ask newlyweds to rate their likelihood of divorce they are most likely to put it at 0 percent. It's also why 90 percent of capital projects have cost overruns (on average 45 percent over their business plan).[17]

Being aware of such biases doesn't help one avoid them. As Dan Ariely, one of the foremost thinkers in the field declares, "I am just as bad myself at making decisions as everyone else I write about."[18] Fortunately, there are a number of proven and practical tools to minimize biases in decision-making including, among others, the following: the "pre-mortem" (generating a list of potential causes for failure of a recommendation and working backwards to rectify them before they happen); "red team-blue team" (assigning one person/group to argue for, and one to argue against, a decision); "clean sheet redesign" (developing a system from only a set of requirements, free from considerations related to current investments or path): and "vanishing options" (taking the preferred option off the table and asking, "what would we do now?"). While there are many tools to choose from, simply engaging a diverse team will reap many of the same decision-making rewards—which research reveals can improve decision-making quality by more than 50 percent.[19]

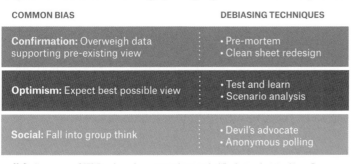

COMMON BIAS	DEBIASING TECHNIQUES
Confirmation: Overweigh data supporting pre-existing view	• Pre-mortem • Clean sheet redesign
Optimism: Expect best possible view	• Test and learn • Scenario analysis
Social: Fall into group think	• Devil's advocate • Anonymous polling

Examples of common biases and related debiasing techniques

#1 In a survey of 772 Board members, respondents ranked "reducing decision biases" as their No. 1 aspiration for improving performance

How do I make it happen?

FOLLOW A **FIVE-STEP PROCESS** TO IMPROVE DECISION-MAKING

A MULTINATIONAL retailer was peering over the abyss. The days of large and established players in the industry coming out on top were numbered—they were entering an era where the nimblest would win. The company, primarily active in mature, low-growth markets and channels, was particularly vulnerable in an increasingly digital world. A new strategy was to be pursued: omni-channel, growing in key emerging markets, finding new sources of differentiation. Virtually all leaders got excited about the potential of the new strategy. The elephant in the room, however, was that the bureaucracy, complexity, and politics of the company stood steadfastly in the face of execution. As a cut-through measure, the executive team commissioned an effort to dramatically increase decision-making effectiveness.

1. Aspire

FIRST, THEY identified the key decisions related to executing the new strategy and prioritized them based on the value at stake and perceived pain (lack of efficiency and effectiveness) in getting the decisions made. Those that rose to the top of the list were ones related to: omni-channel assortment offerings and service levels; developing a cohesive real estate and store-planning strategy; and creating global talent management (in particular expat assignments and growing local talent pools). In total, ten decisions were selected.

Simultaneously, they worked on creating a shared language for what good decision-making looked like. The working team looked at a number of models including the RACI model, and ultimately decided to adapt it to create their own "CDI" model—for any decision. There needed to be up-front role clarification regarding who to Consult during the process of forming a recommendation, who actually Decides the course of action, and who was expected to Implement the decision. Finally, meeting norms were established such as "no prep, no meeting," "starting strong" (by asking what decisions needed to be made and what was the CDI related to the decision), and "three's a charm" (separating the roles of the facilitator, the decision-maker, and the devil's advocate).

Aspire
Where do we want to go?

Align: Create a shared language and aspiration for what good decision-making processes look like

Identify: Determine which decisions bring the highest value for the organization and which are the most inefficient and ineffective

Prioritize: Select the 10-15 most important decision-making processes to improve

2. Assess

HAVING IDENTIFIED the priorities, each decision was mapped to identify the current approach and pain points. Fact-finding on the current process looked at the steps, time spent, meetings held, inputs used, constraints (real and assumed), and roles played. Pain-point exploration asked about frustrations, bottlenecks, drivers of time spent, waste, accuracy, strengths/what works, change suggestions, and barriers to making changes.

Armed with these insights, a "mirror" was created regarding the current state and the list of improvement ideas assembled. Cross-cutting issues were flagged such as the cultural tendency to value "keeping the peace" vs. "telling it like it is" and structural and incentive impediments to collaboration (e.g. the importance of creating an omni-channel merchant role) came into sharp relief, as did the need to provide top-down role clarity as to "who can make the call" on various topics in the matrix.

Finally, the decisions were categorized into three types: those that were infrequent, but high-stakes (which included some key technology, structure, and private-label-related decisions); those that were repetitive and cross-cutting (requiring a process redesign—which included things like category planning, capital planning, and budgeting); and those that were repetitive, but could be delegated (none of which rose to the high-value list).

Assess
How ready are we to go there?

Map: Map the top 10-15 decisions to identify pain points

Root cause: Determine the underlying cause of pain points (process, culture, data, participation, etc.)

Triage: Apply the type A, B, C, framework to determine the most effective approach to address root causes

3. Architect

FOR EACH priority, a decision-making "hot-house" session was then conducted. These sessions took place over two days, involving a diverse representation from all of the stakeholders, and with the purpose of co-creating a significantly more effective approach to making the decision (or, in the case of the one-off decisions—getting the actual decision made) while simultaneously building participants' decision-making capability by practicing numerous de-biasing techniques.

On day one of the session, the participants "looked in the mirror" at the mapping of the current process, its pain points, and the identified root causes. Aided by input from the assessment phase and expertly facilitated, the group then took part in a clean-sheet redesign with the goal of getting to twice the impact in half the time. For the IT capital planning process, for example, this led to solutions such as pushing decisions under $500,000 back into individual businesses, matching approval timing with the release of funds, reducing the application process from thirty pages to one, and adjusting the voting process to reflect the desired future footprint of the business (omni-channel) vs. its current state (heavily weighted to physical channels).

By the end of day one, the new process, roles, and accountabilities were clear (no one was allowed to go home until this was the case!). On day two, the group "ran water through the pipes"—pressure-testing the new approach in a role-play format to determine how much time was really saved, what incremental impact was achieved, and how the decision could be improved. A pre-mortem was then conducted to ask the question, "If in a year the pain points have returned, why would that have been the case?" This, then, led to a structured reflection on the mindset and behavior shifts and commitments required to make the new process work (or in the case of the one-off decisions, to ensure implementation happened). Next steps were then clarified.

In parallel with the hot-house sessions, the senior team convened to make decisions related to the cross-cutting issues found in the assess stage (structural, cultural, incentive, etc.) and HR and communications worked together to develop a decision-making excellence and skill-building campaign to roll out broadly.

Architect
What do we need to do to get there?

Clean sheet: Redesign key decision-making processes using a clean-sheet approach (how do we get 2x quality in half the time?)

Role play: Dry-run contentious decisions through the new processes to refine the design

De-bias: Apply de-biasing techniques to further test and refine suggested changes

Integrated plan: Create an implementation plan that addresses the process and cultural changes needed to make improvements happen

4. Act

IN THE FOLLOWING weeks and months, the solutions developed during the "hot-house" sessions were methodically put into practice, as were the other, broader changes agreed to by the top team. The project team that had led the effort stayed intact, overseeing implementation, including playing a "referee" role in the execution of the new process. As wins were achieved (including the hiring of a new group of world-class omni-channel merchants, the alignment of incentives across the e-commerce and physical channels teams, and moving from allocating capital based on historic usage to value-creation potential, and doing so in half the time previously), they were communicated broadly to create pull from the organization to learn and apply more in relation to decision-making effectiveness.

The effort worked. Not only did the CDI language take hold, but there was significant pull for the Do-It-Yourself versions of the "hot-house" approach which included step-by-step methods for prioritizing decisions, understanding the current state, uncovering pain points, applying redesign levers, pressure-testing new approaches, and measuring effectiveness. When applied deeper in the organization, more and more of the repetitive, lower-stakes-type decisions made the priority list, and in turn were dealt with by delegation to the lowest level possible—dramatically increasing the sense of empowerment deeper down in the organization and freeing up meaningful leadership time to focus on other issues.

Act
How do we manage the journey?

Governance: Put in place clear governance to ensure recommendations move from words on a page to espoused practices in the organization

Capability building: Provide a superstructure to ensure the new design process works first time around

Reinforcement: Send strong and visible messages that leaders value everyone's efforts in making changes

5. Advance

ONCE THE program was well on track, the working team turned its sights to creating a simple, non-bureaucratic, decision-making dashboard to enable the pulse to be kept on decision-making effectiveness in the organization.

The company's e-mail and calendar software was used to unobtrusively take stock of the amount of time and people involved in various decisions. A five-question "pulse survey" was also used in key decision areas to highlight any backsliding or further improvement potential.

Finally, the company's on-boarding and capability-building approaches were enhanced to include modules on decision-making effectiveness, covering everything from the CDI model to expected meeting norms and related mindsets and behaviors, and the various tools available to improve decision-making processes.

Advance
How do we keep moving forward?

Measure: Rigorously take stock of effectiveness and efficiency improvements

Learn: Codify best practices and share them with other applicable areas

Institutionalize: Ensure that a company approach exists so that clean decision-making processes are created for new decisions that arise (to prevent pain points from emerging)

LESS THAN A YEAR after they had confronted their decision-making challenges, the senior team shared a genuine feeling that the effort had "unstuck" the organization. Important decisions had been made about the company's operating model that ended the stand-off between the digital and physical businesses. The pace and speed of progress against key strategic priorities had picked up significantly. Perhaps most gratifying was the constructive dialogue taking place across the organization that was removing decision-making barriers as they cropped up—unconstructive meetings were "called out" and changes made on the spot, and unclear accountabilities were raised, escalated, and resolved quickly.

DECISION-MAKING:
AT A GLANCE

WHY IS IT IMPORTANT?

- Decision quality can make or break a company.
- Poor decision-making is rampant.
- It affects your ability to retain talent.

WHAT ARE THE BIG IDEAS?

- Differentiate among three types of decisions.
- Dialogue is as (or more) important than data.
- Watch out for biases.

HOW DO I MAKE IT HAPPEN?

- Follow a five-step process to improve decision-making.

  Most commonly neglected action in each step:

  Aspire: Prioritize efforts based on value and "pain."

  Assess: Fully understand root causes in problem-areas.

  Architect: Clean sheet solve for at least 2x improvement.

  Act: "Dry run" solutions with all stakeholders before going live.

  Advance: Institutionalize stock takes/continuous improvement.

Chapter 6

How do I reorganize to capture maximum value quickly?

We acknowledge McKinsey Senior Partner Aaron DeSmet
for his work in co-authoring this chapter.

Organization redesign:
A TIMELESS TOPIC

THE HISTORY OF ORGANIZATIONS is as long as the history of humankind. Without organization, it's unlikely the human race would have survived in a hostile, prehistoric world. By organizing ourselves to work together towards common goals, our organizations achieve feats that go far beyond anything that individuals could accomplish alone. Whether it's the mass-produced products and services we use on a daily basis, public transport, space travel, the Internet, or the mapping of the human genome, almost everything we see and experience is the result of human organization.

Every generation searches for better, more efficient and effective ways to organize themselves to achieve their goals. During this evolution we've moved from models centered on a strong leader with absolute power in family/tribal units, to the hierarchical, pyramid structures with clear divisions of labor in early political and business empires, to matrixed and cross-functional structures promoting more complex forms of collaboration and value creation. Based on the many experiments happening today, many believe that we are on the verge of another major evolutionary step in the form of more decentralized, adaptive, and even self-organizing approaches.

One of the most high-profile experiments is that of Zappos, the online shoe and clothing retailer, which announced in 2013 that it would adopt a holarchy. In a holarchy there are no job titles or permanent roles (instead roles are fluidly rearranged based on peer agreement). There is also full transparency of information (in this case using a web-based tracker of all strategy decisions and their outcomes called GlassFrog). Philosophically, the approach has its roots in Frédéric Laloux's book, *Reinventing Organizations*, which describes this approach as "the next stage of human consciousness...taming our ego and searching for more authentic, more wholesome ways of being."[1]

Time will determine whether the Zappos experiment will address the issues confronting more traditional organization designs that holocracy is trying to solve, or whether studies by academics that suggest such elimination of hierarchy is disorienting and impractical (resulting in an unmanageable bureaucracy) will be proven true in practice.[2] Whatever the outcome, we believe that it won't be the end of the story—organization design will continue to evolve as long as humans are here to organize. Holding a different view would be akin to the apocryphal statement attributed to Charles H. Duell, Commissioner of the U.S. Patent office, in 1899, "Everything that can be invented has been invented."[3]

We also believe that the days of being able to say "under X circumstances (e.g. size of organization, competitive environment, strategy, technology available), organization archetype Y will lead to optimal performance (e.g. by product, function, geography, project, process)" are over. There is too much change across too many variables in the twenty-first century for such an approach to be effective. Instead, we offer our best thinking to help you find the right design specific to your organization, which will likely be a combination of traditional and experimental organizational structures, formal and informal ways of operating, and fluidity and stability of design.

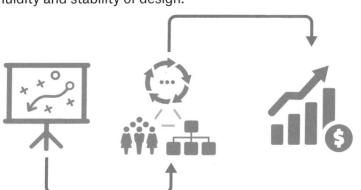

Organization design is the plan for how a company distributes and coordinates activities and information flows to deliver desired outcomes

Why is it important?

REDESIGN IS **INEVITABLE**

ACCORDING TO a recent survey, up to 82 percent of executives say they have experienced a significant organization redesign at either the corporate, functional, or business unit level in their current companies. What's more, 70 percent of these report that the most recent reorganizations were implemented during the past two years. Further, the majority of executives believe that they will again experience a redesign in the next two years.[4] This may be surprising to some, but when you consider that the average time in role for a business executive is just over two years, that almost 50 percent of executives new in role launch some kind of reorganization, and that most CEO's have nearly ten direct reports, it's not hard to see how this is the case.[5,6,7] Large-scale organization redesigns, it would appear, happen more often than a company redesigns its website (on average every three years) or upgrades its computer systems (typically every 3–5 years).

The implications of this are staggering, in particular when one considers that an average reorganization takes ten months to go from plan to practice, and that more than half of executives report that they see a dip in productivity during its implementation.[8] Perhaps an apt analogy, albeit far less emotionally charged, is that of driving a new car. Cars, like organizations, are designed for a specific purpose. A minivan is designed to move a family around efficiently and comfortably. A sports car is designed to look good and accelerate quickly. A sports utility vehicle is designed for payload space and to handle off-road conditions. If you're used to driving one of these vehicles, it takes time to adjust to another: the sensitivity of the pedals, the turning radius, the blind spots, which side the fuel cap is on, the position of the turn signal indicators and the windshield wipers, how to adjust the seats, and so on. Now imagine if it took, on average, ten driving hours to get fully comfortable driving it, and then, after driving it for only twenty-four hours, you decided to change vehicles into a different car class altogether! Why would you do it?

The answer is that you wouldn't. Unless of course, the function you needed from your vehicle changed significantly. The organizational equivalent is a change of strategy driven by the increasing pace of technology disruptions, new market opportunities, changes in customer preferences, or competitor moves. Wherever small, incremental tweaks won't cut it, big bang shake-ups are required. The accelerated pace of such changes in today's business environment no doubt contributes to the frequency of redesigns. It also, however, puts a premium on speeding up the time from plan to practice (else we'll be changing vehicles faster than we can get up to speed driving them!).

It's not all about navigating a changing external landscape, however—you'd also change out your vehicle if you weren't satisfied with its current performance on the road you were on. As we'll discuss later in this chapter, this dynamic is also clearly at play. Any way you look at it, management thinker David Ulrich is right: "As [organization design] happens more and more, every leader needs to know how to do it well."[9] Redesign is inevitable; embrace it, plan for it.

Frequency and duration of organization redesigns

82% of executives say they have experienced a significant organization redesign

70% of those report that their most recent reorganizations were implemented during the past two years

The average reorganization takes **10 MONTHS** from plan to practice

"As [organization design] happens more and more, every leader needs to know how to do it well."
Management thinker David Ulrich

Why is it important?
REDESIGNS CAN HAVE PROFOUND IMPACT

EXECUTIVES LOOKING to redesign their organizations have high hopes. Nearly two-thirds report that their most recent redesigns sought to facilitate execution of their strategic priorities, more than half say their redesigns aimed to improve the focus on growth. Rounding out the top five reasons are improving decision-making (40 percent), cost-cutting (39 percent), and accountability (39 percent). [10]

When redesigns deliver, the impact is profound. Consider how growth potential was unlocked by Indian multinational IT services company HCL Technologies' founder, Shiv Nadar, when he verticalized operations and enabled increased specialization to meet the demands of its target industries. Or how the CEO of Ford, Alan Mulally, used organization redesign to unlock the leadership team's ability to make critical enterprise decisions better and faster, which led to the previously problematic creation of global car platforms.

The merits of a redesign are often difficult to judge, however, as a redesign that creates significant value in one context or era may lead to decline in the next. Consider the fortunes of Zurich-based power technology and automation company, ABB. In 1990, CEO Percy Barnevik chose to pursue a radical decentralization. The idea was to unleash local entrepreneurship by "ripping down bureaucracy" so that employees all over the world could launch new products, change designs, and alter production methods "without meddling from headquarters." [11] The structure itself was a matrix of sectors and countries that was then divided into 5,000 profit centers. As profits soared, the structure was highly praised by academics, journalists, management gurus, and shareholders. By 1996, ABB was named Europe's most respected company for the third year in a row by the *Financial Times*.

Fast-forward to the turn of the century when revenue growth was slowing at an alarming rate and the share price began to nose-dive. As customers had become multinational and competitors more sophisticated, the once-praised design was now being derided for being a contributor to ABB's fall. As one reporter wrote, "the decentralized management structure Mr. Barnevick created for the company's far-flung units ended up causing conflicts and communications problems between departments." Dysfunctional competition festered and enormous duplication created massive inefficiencies (by way of example, at the time ABB had 576 enterprise resource planning (ERP) systems, sixty different payroll systems, and more than 600 spreadsheet software programs!).[12] By this time even Barnevick was willing to concede that the organization design was "good [in the past], but it is not good today."[13]

In 2002, new CEO Jürgen Dormann significantly redesigned the organization by consolidating divisions and centralizing profit-and-loss accountability. More efficient and better able to collaborate to generate fast, competitive bids for multinational clients, the company's fortunes were turned around.

The moral of the story? Getting design right has big upsides and downsides; be wary that the very same design may bring you both over time.

% OF EXECUTIVES CITING DESIRED BENEFIT

Improved strategic focus	62
Growth	53
Better decision-making	40
Cost-cutting	39
Improved accountability	39

Benefits sought from organizational redesign by senior executives

"In every phase of our strategy change, we have paved the way by altering organizational structures and our ways of working"
J. V. Knudstorp, CEO, Lego

Why is it important?
ONLY 23 PERCENT
GET IT RIGHT

THERE IS AN APHORISM that says, "Your organization is perfectly designed to give you the business results that you have today, so if you want to improve results you should redesign your organization." Many leaders find this very appealing, but is it as simple as this in practice? Unfortunately not.

American writer Charlton Ogburn Jr. captured what happens in the majority of cases when he wrote, "We tend to meet any new situation by reorganizing; and a wonderful method it can be for creating the illusion of progress while producing confusion, inefficiency, and demoralization."[14] Indeed, our most recent survey of executives shows that only 23 percent say their reorganization efforts were a success, meaning that it met their objectives and improved performance.[15]

Breaking it down, 44 percent of reorganizations get bogged down in implementation and are never actually finished. A historic example of this is at Proctor and Gamble. In 1999, CEO Durk Jager inherited an organization that he and other leaders felt was too complacent, not innovative enough, and constrained by a conservative hierarchical structure. In an effort to unlock performance, Jager reorganized the company from a geographic divisional structure into a more decentralized product group structure, giving each group a mandate to develop innovative products to serve customer needs. Although considered a good design on paper, Jager was unable to mobilize the organization, in particular middle managers, to work effectively in the new structure. Had he spent more time getting others on board, his fate of being exited from the CEO role, just eighteen months after he was hired, might have been averted.[16]

Another 23 percent of redesigns are fully implemented, but the objectives of the redesign aren't met. Chrysler restructured its organization three times in three years to little effect, ultimately leading to its bankruptcy and eventual merger with Fiat.

Finally, 10 percent of redesigns have a significant negative impact on performance. Yahoo!'s former CEO Terry Semel reorganized the company into a matrix structure, aiming to improve the sharing of resources across various projects. The result was a drastic lack of accountability and horrible gridlock in decision-making that left Yahoo! far behind its peers in the fast-moving technology industry. As one executive who left the company put it, "The great people leave because they don't feel they have the tools and authority to be successful with what they are notionally responsible for. Or because there are so many people who think they are in charge, they can't get anything done. The mediocre people stay, as they are protected and not held accountable."[17]

Although the number of abject failures is relatively small, we warn that the cumulative effect of anything less than success can be equally detrimental as cycles of reorganization with little impact take the "confusion, inefficiency, and demoralization" that Charlton Ogburn Jr. wrote about and embed them into the company culture.

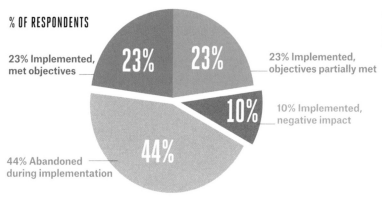

% OF RESPONDENTS

Outcomes of redesign efforts

23% Implemented, met objectives — **23%**

23% — 23% Implemented, objectives partially met

10% — 10% Implemented, negative impact

44% Abandoned during implementation — **44%**

What are the big ideas?

THINK **BEYOND LINES AND BOXES**

NEARLY ONE IN TEN people around the world suffer from lower back pain. It causes more disability than nearly 300 other conditions worldwide and is responsible for about a third of work-related disability.[18] What's the cause? Now that's a fascinating question—in 85 to 90 percent of cases, there is no clear-cut diagnosis.[19] In these cases, patients hear that the primary causes are structural (e.g. spinal stenosis or abnormal facet joints), related to soft-tissue problems, (e.g. a herniated disc, a strained lumbar muscle, a pinched sciatic nerve, or tendonalgia), or are psychological not physical (the result of repressed emotions such as unexpressed anxiety or anger).[20] Some may dismiss the latter, but it's worth noting that studies suggest surgery to address structural issues is successful in 26 percent of patients,[21] whereas physiotherapy and psychological interventions lead to far higher success rates, up to 76 percent in some studies.[22]

The story of lower back pain is an apt analogy for how to think about organization redesign. If you think only about addressing the structural elements, your probability of success will remain low. By structural elements we mean lines and boxes, roles and responsibilities (e.g. functional vs. business), boundaries (e.g. insourcing vs. outsourcing) and location (e.g. location of HQ), and governance (e.g. committee structures). Another category to consider in the redesign is process elements, such as process design (e.g. standardization) and decisions (e.g. decision rights), performance management (e.g. key performance indicators and related rewards), IT and technology enablers (e.g. IT infrastructure), and other linkages (e.g. information flows). The people elements of a redesign, including workforce size, informal networks, skills and talent, and culture, also need considering.

While all these elements account for the way work is done, most leaders find it hard not to gravitate to lines and boxes as their main concern—most often due to its tangibility and the emotional weight employees attach to where they end up in the chart. Other leaders, however, swing the pendulum in the opposite direction and make the design conversation about the people—we've sat through many unproductive discussions along the lines of, "So what if Pierre reported to Francis, how would Abdul feel? Or wait, maybe Ingrid could run the new product line and Abdul could double hat so he doesn't feel he's getting a demotion, and we could give him the strategy group too. Oh, but then when Pierre retires, we need to have Susan ready, and a two-in-a-box role won't prepare her in the eyes of the market..." And on, and on, and on.

Our data suggests that when leaders take into account the dynamic interaction across all three elements described above, they are three times more likely to be successful than those that don't. What's more, it's likely to be a life-changing experience for the workforce, not dissimilar to an individual being cured of chronic back pain!

CATEGORY **LEVER**

STRUCTURE
- Boxes and lines
- Roles and responsibilities
- Boundaries and location
- Governance

PROCESSES
- Process design and decisions
- Performance management
- IT and technology
- Linkages

PEOPLE
- Workforce size
- Informal networks
- Skills and talent
- Culture, behaviors and mindsets

70% of companies use only 1-2 levers

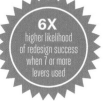

6X higher likelihood of redesign success when 7 or more levers used

Levers for redesigning an organization

What are the big ideas?
AGILITY REQUIRES STABILITY

AUSTRALIAN-BORN media mogul Rupert Murdoch is often credited with saying, "The world is changing very fast. Big will not beat small anymore. It will be the fast beating the slow." This makes for a great sound bite (as you'd expect from a media man!), but fast doesn't really help if you're headed to the wrong destination. We'd argue that the real advantage lies in being agile, not just fast. What's the difference? Agility involves not just speed, but balance, coordination, strength, stamina, and reflexes. You can get speed by doing the same thing, only faster. Agility is smarter and more graceful—and knows when being first isn't about being fast (the adage "the second mouse gets the cheese" sums up the sentiment).

Columbia Business School professor Rita Gunther McGrath's research sheds light on an agile organization's look and feel. She found that large companies that disproportionately grow their income vs. others have two main characteristics: "On the one hand, [growth companies] are built for innovation, [they are] good at experimentation [and] can move on a dime. On the other hand, they're extremely stable, [the] strategy and organization structure stay consistent [and the] culture is strong and unchanging."[23] Our research confirms this: companies that are both fast and stable are over three times more likely to be high-performing than those that are fast, but lack stable operating disciplines.

The power of this idea shouldn't be underestimated. Most leaders see the speed and flexibility that drives innovation at the opposite end of the spectrum from standardization and centralization which drive efficiency and control risk. This is a false trade-off. Perhaps an apt analogy is that of society at large, where individual freedom is at one end of the spectrum and government control is at the other. Yet they need each other: without submission to and enforcement of the law, a free society would become anarchy.

In practical terms: to be agile, leaders should determine which parts of their organization design are stable and unchanging and, at the same time, create looser, more dynamic elements that can be adapted quickly to new challenges and opportunities. Using a smartphone analogy, you need to choose your hardware and operating system first (stability), and then let go of control so that useful apps can be developed and improved (agility). So, for example, you might choose a primary axis of organization (stability) while facilitating the formation of temporary performance cells around solving specific needs (speed). Or standardize work in a few signature processes (stability) and coordinate work through iterative cycles in other areas (speed). Or you could emphasize a set of shared cultural values (stability) while radically empowering the front line to make decisions in keeping with these values (speed).

Companies with an agile organization design have another relatively unique feature: They break the cycle of going through large-scale organization redesigns every couple of years. Why? They achieve a state of continuous reorganization around a stable core.

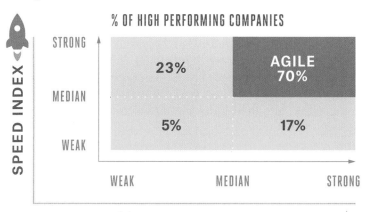

Relationship between speed and stability to performance

What are the big ideas?
FOLLOW **NINE GOLDEN RULES**

THERE'S A RULE in the hotel at which you are staying that says no one is to take a shower between 10 pm and 6 am. The catch is that it's 10:05 pm and you've just arrived, having flown from overseas and slept on an airplane. You've got a 6 am meeting. Do you follow the rule? The next morning you pull your rental car out of the parking lot and instinctually drive on the right-hand side of the road—and suddenly you remember that in this country the rule is that you drive on the left. Do you change lanes?

Rules are generally meant to protect us from negative consequences. Yet we don't always follow them, adopting a "rules are made to be broken" stance. On the other hand, sometimes it's crazy not to follow the rules. To paraphrase Spanish novelist Carlos Ruiz Zafón, you don't win a game of tennis by hitting the ball out of the court.[24] When it comes to redesigning your organization, research shows there are nine rules that are well worth following. When you do, your redesign is more than seven times more likely to succeed than if you only follow a few. Even if all of the rules aren't followed, the more that are, the higher the chances of success.[25] The nine rules are:

RULE #1 Focus first on the longer-term strategic aspirations—a focus only on pain points typically results in unforeseen new ones being created.

RULE #2 Take time to survey the scene—create an accurate and verifiable picture of today's structure, process, and people.

RULE #3 Be structured about selecting the right blueprint—create multiple options and test them under various scenarios.

RULE #4 Go beyond lines and boxes—we deemed this rule so important that we've already talked about it as one of our "big ideas"!

RULE #5 Be rigorous about drafting in talent—create a talent draft that enables well-defined roles at each level to be filled in an orderly and transparent fashion.

RULE #6 Identify the necessary mind-set shifts, and change those mind-sets—don't assume people will automatically fall in line and follow instructions.

RULE #7 Establish metrics that measure short-term and long-term success—run what is a major human capital project with the same rigor as a major capital project.

RULE #8 Make sure business leaders communicate—create a powerful narrative around the redesign and cascade it through the company in an interactive way.

RULE #9 Manage the transitional risks—monitor and mitigate risks (e.g. interruptions to business continuity, talent loss, customer care lapses); i.e. jump with a parachute!

In the high stakes game of redesigning your organization, we advise playing by the rules!

% OF REDESIGNS

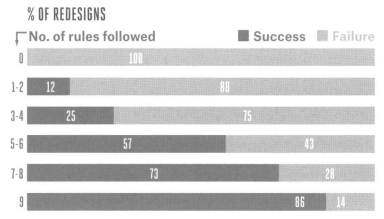

No. of rules followed	Success	Failure
0		100
1-2	12	88
3-4	25	75
5-6	57	43
7-8	73	28
9	86	14

Correlation between successful redesigns and use of the nine golden rules

How do I make it happen?

FOLLOW A **FIVE-STEP PROCESS** TO SUCCESSFULLY REORGANIZE

A large U.S.-based chemical company found itself consistently being outmaneuvered by smaller, more agile competitors. The company had grown significantly over the previous decades, but growth had stalled. The CEO and top team decided on a new strategy to regain market share with more specialized products and increasing quality and service in target customer segments. It was clear to the senior team that executing their new strategy would require a new organization design.

1. Aspire

THE FIRST STEP was to fully articulate the organizational requirements of the new strategy. The conversation kicked off with a top-team session where they agreed the company needed to dramatically strengthen functional capabilities (and in particular commercial capabilities) and unlock more innovation than they'd been able to deliver in the past. They also needed to clarify accountabilities so that functional leaders would know how to make trade-offs between competing demands, and so sales reps would know who could make decisions on specific customer requests. Further, complexity created by the current matrix of product lines, functions, and geographies needed simplifying. This had particular impact on the sales area where customers typically had two or three sales reps calling on them in a largely uncoordinated manner (and key accounts spanning multiple geographies could end up being called upon by ten reps!).

The senior team had learned from previous failed redesigns that if they didn't get the voice of a broader leadership coalition in the mix early, the effort would be doomed to fail. The answer wouldn't be as good and, more importantly, the ownership for making it happen would be low. As such, a highly collaborative and transparent approach was taken to refine the design requirements. Leaders several levels down and high potential talent from each area were engaged in a series of workshops to debate and refine the draft set of principles. Ultimately they agreed on a set that included, among others: creating a single point of contact for priority customers, delegating decisions to the lowest level possible, choosing a primary axis in the matrix, clarifying accountabilities and making explicit protocols for handovers in cross-functional processes, and allowing for agile project team structures to serve ad hoc missions as they emerge.

Aspire
Where do we want to go?

Strategic requirements: Determine implications of the business strategy for organization design

Pain points: Identify what isn't working well in the current structure

Design principles: Synthesize strategy and pain points into specific criteria to guide design

Engagement model: Identify which leaders should be involved, and when, and the rules of engagement

2. Assess

BEFORE TURNING the principles into specific blueprints, an accurate baseline of the current organization was put together. This turned out to be a surprisingly difficult task. Instead of an easy "drag and drop" exercise from HR systems, the data pull revealed many issues: blank data fields and information that just hadn't been kept up to date. Vague job categories made it difficult to understand what roles people actually played, and overlapping structures double-counted a number of roles. The number of employees in each area and overall didn't add up.

Once the data was scrubbed, internal and external benchmarks were explored. While remaining aware of the limitations of benchmarking, it was instructive to find staffing levels were at least 20–30 percent higher than the industry average. Also, as they looked externally at other research and development departments, they realized just how far away their complex and rigid structure was from the "innovation engine" they needed for the future. By interviewing key customers, they heard first-hand what was needed for a consistent, integrated sales approach. It wasn't all bad news, though, as there were a number of strengths to protect and amplify: the company had some of the industry's best technical talent in manufacturing and R&D, an in-depth knowledge of the customer needs within their sales force, and a metrics-driven performance culture—important assets that they needed to capitalize on for the future.

The next step was to translate the agreed upon principles into a concrete set of options, taking into account the baseline and existing strengths of the organization. These were pressure-tested against a set of industry scenarios and a "red team, blue team" decision-making approach (a debate format where one team only argues the pros, and the other the cons). Ultimately the set was narrowed from ten to three for presentation to the senior team, who would then decide which one to recommend to the board.

Assess
How ready are we to go there?

Baseline: Develop an accurate, quantitative baseline for your organization

Strengths: Understand the strengths of your structure that should be retained

Benchmarks: Assess structure against best practice to determine further opportunity

Design options: Develop a range of potential structures and test them against design principles

3. Architect

AFTER A ROBUST debate, the senior team decided on a top-level design that made the functional axis primary. All operational activities would go under a new COO; sales staff who were currently distributed across different product groups and regions were pulled together under a Chief Commercial Officer; a new research and development function would be elevated to the top team as a direct report to the CEO. Complementing this stable backbone was an agile organizational overlay that enabled pools of functional talent to be drawn on and staffed into working teams to address complex customer and internal issues as they emerged (in what was referred to as a "flow-to-work" staffing model). These SWAT-type groups were to be funded, empowered, held accountable, and decommissioned in up to three-month intervals, encouraging rapid iteration and closure on issues. The overall design was pressure-tested with key customers and regulators, and then taken to the board where it received unanimous support.

The next step was a series of workshops involving selected staff at lower levels to determine how the new structure would work in practice for each key function. The groups went through a similar (though abbreviated) approach to the one that led to the top-level design: understanding the principles, baseline, and strengths; developing and pressure-testing detailed options, and then making a final decision. Once the detailed work had been done in each area, all of the pieces were put together and final adjustments made to ensure they were harmonized. When the senior team had approved it, the final design was given to the HR team who compiled a list of critical positions with their specific requirements (including skills, behaviors, and mindsets). The final step was the design of a rigorous talent-matching process, guided by a playbook to ensure fairness and transparency.

Architect
What do we need to do to get there?

High-level design: Make tradeoffs, pick a primary axis (the stable backbone) and mechanisms for agility, finalize your high-level design choice

Sign-off: Ensure the board and key stakeholders sign off on the design

Detailed design and testing: Define in detail the related changes needed in structure, process and people

Talent redraft: Use a rigorous process to place talent in the new organization

4. Act

IN PARALLEL with determining who would fill key leadership roles in the new structure, a rollout plan was developed. The plan involved a CEO announcement of the redesign to the broader organization followed by an orchestrated series of cascading workshops to enable the senior and middle managers to understand the structure, process, and people implications overall for their area, and for them as individuals. Conversations with those leaders who were most affected were to happen before the announcement and included one-on-ones from the board, CEO, and top team. A Program Management Office (PMO) was set up to coordinate the process, ensure that critical milestones would be met, and monitor customer satisfaction, employee engagement, and retention.

One of the most important elements of the rollout plan was the mindset and behavior shifts needed for the new design to work in practice. Leaders would have to become far more comfortable being held accountable for things that were not directly in their control. They would have to accept that some customers would receive less service than in the past, given the segmentation strategy. They would have to share knowledge—not protect it as their edge to get the next promotion. Actions to influence these shifts were built into the rollout plan and included role modeling, communications, skill-building, and changes to processes, systems, and incentives.

Act
How do we manage the journey?

"From-to" mindsets: Identify any needed shifts in mindsets needed to support the future design

Rollout plan: Develop plan to cascade detailed design and day one launch, incorporating rapid iteration and refinement of agile elements

Communications plan: Develop external and internal communications approach by stakeholder

Support infrastructure: Ensure sponsorship, PMO, metrics, and tracking mechanisms are in place

5. Advance

GIVEN THEIR extensive involvement in the design, leadership buy-in was high throughout the rollout. Involving and informing staff in a transparent manner meant there was less anxiety and confusion in the organization compared to previous reorganizations. Feedback from customers and other key external stakeholders continued to be positive, in part because such care was taken to ensure business continuity throughout the implementation. This positivity also fueled an ability to attract high-quality talent from the outside with desired profiles—bringing both needed capability and positively influencing the desired mindset and behavior shifts. Not everything went according to plan, but the PMO structure was quick to identify and address issues as they emerged.

Advance
How do we keep moving forward?

Execution monitoring: Monitor transition to primary axis and agile scale ups against key operational and financial metrics and milestones

Talent management: Take steps to retain top talent and attract external talent

Business continuity: Safeguard key processes for customer servicing and performance reporting

Employee engagement: Ensure employees feel supported and address their concerns

---

AFTER A YEAR of working in the new structure, the company was back on a positive growth trajectory—the strategy was working, as was the organization design that supported it. Choosing a functional primary axis had been the right call, and the talent placed in key positions was working out well together. The organization had broken through on the agility front—the new structure had allowed them to successfully create empowered, cross-functional teams to deliver against key market opportunities. Ideas about how to provide more value to customers were no longer stalled by the bureaucracy. Instead, they were quickly put to the test, and if they succeeded they were scaled. In the words of the CEO, "We didn't find a silver bullet...but we found a way to manufacture all the ammunition we need to win!"

ORGANIZATION REDESIGN:
AT A GLANCE

WHY IS IT IMPORTANT?

- Redesign is inevitable.
- Redesigns can have profound impact.
- Only 23 percent get it right.

WHAT ARE THE BIG IDEAS?

- Think beyond lines and boxes.
- Agility requires stability.
- Follow nine golden rules.

HOW DO I MAKE IT HAPPEN?

- Follow a five-step process to successfully reorganize.

  Most commonly neglected action in each step:

  Aspire: Solve for strategic needs, not just pain points.

  Assess: Ensure your baseline is bullet-proof.

  Architect: Explicitly pick a primary (stable) axis.

  Act: Rapidly iterate agile design elements.

  Advance: Safeguard business continuity from day one.

7

Chapter

How do I reduce overhead costs sustainably?

Overhead Cost Reduction:
A TIMELESS TOPIC

IN JOSEPH TAINTER'S *The Collapse of Complex Societies*, he reviews more than two dozen cases of societal collapse during the last 2,000 years, and in doing so he posits that human societies are problem-solving organizations. But, over time, responses to problems add layers of organizational complexity and there comes a point when the cost of complexity overtakes the benefit, causing the system to collapse.[1] Edward Gibbon, in *The Decline and Fall of the Roman Empire*, echoes Tainter's assertion, characterizing that a meaningful part of the Empire's fall was the result of "The number of ministers, of magistrates, of officers, and of servants, who filled different departments of the state... multiplied beyond former times." He concludes that a swollen bureaucracy that required excessive taxation to maintain it became "intolerable"—causing revolt.[2]

These accounts may as well have been studies of modern mega-companies. A business is a problem-solving organization. As it grows, it faces new challenges in its environment and responds by adding increased complexity to its management system—systems, controls, processes, meetings to ensure all the variables can be managed. These systems and processes then take on a life of their own, and more time is spent leading and maintaining them (sitting in meetings, filling out forms, updating presentations) than is spent directly working on products and services that benefit customers. If this cycle continues, the costs of running the business grow such that the prices are no longer competitive—causing customers (and talent) to revolt.

While a full solution to issues such as excessive bureaucracy and organizational complexity requires applying tools/techniques that cut across the topics we cover in this book (e.g. decision-making effectiveness, culture change, organization design, performance management, transformational change), one physical manifestation of complexity and bureaucracy in organizations is in overhead costs. By overhead we mean the costs involved in running the company versus those directly involved in making a product or delivering a service. These costs are often referred to as "fixed" (don't change with volumes of products or services sold), which means that trimming them decreases the revenues necessary to make a profit, and if and when they get out of control they can sink the business.

Howard Schultz, CEO of Starbucks, reminds us, "You can't cut enough costs to save your way to prosperity."[3] At the same time, it's important for any company to ensure it keeps its overhead costs in check. After all, each dollar earned in sales contributes a small percentage in profit, but each dollar saved goes directly to the bottom line. An apt analogy is that of "Spring Cleaning" one's home—every year low-value, redundant, obsolete items are removed from closets, pantries, and garages, and what remains is reorganized to be useful. Inevitably, however, things pile up over the ensuing year, and the same ritual is required annually—or else one's house can too easily become a candidate for *Hoarders* (the U.S. documentary series depicting the real-life struggles of those unwilling to discard what they've acquired)! But is there a way to break the cycle of periodically cutting and then seeing it all grow back to then cut again? Read on to find out...

PRODUCTION-RELATED COSTS, E.G.

- raw material
- production line labor
- consumable supplies

OVERHEAD COSTS, E.G.

- sales & marketing
- facilities
- accounting & legal

Overhead costs are those involved in running the company vs. those directly related to making a product or delivering a service

 "A penny saved is a penny earned"—Benjamin Franklin, 1737

Why is it important?
VALUE CREATING COMPANIES KEEP COSTS UNDER CONTROL

IN ACCOUNTING STATEMENTS, overhead costs mostly show up in the line item of "General and Administrative" costs (G&A). Across the S&P Global 1200 index, G&A costs account for an estimated US$1.8 trillion annually. Against this backdrop, in the words of McKinsey's Alison Watkins and Robert Levin, "If there has ever been an earnings presentation where a CEO was asked why G&A expenses were too low, we have yet to see it. On the contrary, it's practically a truism that reducing the cost of support functions will improve profitability and let management put the savings to more productive use—or return at least a portion of the savings to shareholders."[4] What's more, McKinsey research has also found that keeping G&A expenses in check is the second largest predictor among the factors studied of becoming a top-quartile economic-value creator.[5]

It's not surprising, then, to find out that 68 percent of CEOs report they plan to introduce cost-cutting initiatives in the next twelve months.[6] Yet many leaders feel these efforts will ultimately be fruitless—40 percent of executives report strong concern that cost reduction programs pursued will see the same costs creep back in twelve to eighteen months.[7] Is this concern warranted? Not only are they being sensible, the data suggests they are overly optimistic!

A study looking at S&P Global 1200 companies that announced cost reductions over a seven-year period, assessing the extent to which savings were not just achieved for the first year, but sustained for three years after, shows that only one in four were able to do so (with no correlations found to industry, size, geography, or performance relative to peers).[8] Another study showed that while companies in the U.S. cut on average 18 percent of their G&A costs during the financial crisis, afterwards a full 60 percent of business executives still believed their organization's support functions were ineffective, cost too much, or both.[9] Previous studies have shown even more depressing results, finding that only 10 percent of G&A reduction efforts show sustained results three years later.[10]

In many ways, the relationship between organizations and overhead cost is not dissimilar to the relationship between people and weight loss. Nearly 30 percent of the global population qualifies as overweight or obese (with more than 30 percent in emerging markets).[11] The most common way of losing weight globally—making a change in one's diet—sees nearly 65 percent of dieters return to their pre-dieting weight within three years.[12] For dieters who lose weight rapidly, the results are even worse, with 95 percent of people regaining the weight, and sometimes more, within a few months or years.[13]

If you listen to the weight-loss industry, you'll hear many claims about how easy it is to lose weight: just take this pill, follow that diet, buy this piece of equipment, and everything melts away in a flash. Significant investment of time and resources later, people are still overweight. Similarly, leaders too often think that quick fixes—looking at aggregate numbers, applying blanket targets, and simple rules of thumb—will lead to realizable, lasting, and significant benefits. They won't.

IT'S IMPORTANT

Keeping overhead in check is the second largest predictor of value creation

"If there has ever been an earnings presentation where a CEO was asked why G&A expenses were too low, we have yet to see it."
– McKinsey Quarterly

IT'S HARD

25% of cost reduction programs sustain savings for three years

"There is no evidence that cutting to improve profitability helps beyond the immediate, short-term accounting bump."
– Wharton Center for Human Resources

The opportunity and challenge of overhead cost reduction

Why is it important?
DONE POORLY, IT
SABOTAGES FUTURE GROWTH

USING DIETING as an analogy for cost-cutting is instructive on many levels. Consider, for example, research done by Rockefeller University that looked at the effect of different daily calorie reductions on weight loss. At one level, the research showed what you'd expect—the fewer calories you consume, the more weight you lose (as in business where the more areas you find to cut, the lower your cost base will be). Not obvious, however, was where the weight-loss came from in different scenarios. For those who only moderately reduced their daily caloric intake, 91 percent of the weight loss was from fat and the remaining 9 percent from muscle. On the other hand, those who severely reduced their daily intake experienced a full 42 percent of their weight loss from muscle![14]

Looking deeper into the dynamics at play, as the body loses more muscle mass, its metabolic rate decreases (a resting muscle burns almost eight times more energy than a fat cell). This accounts for why other studies have shown that diets that involve a simple 200 calorie-per-day reduction result in the same sustainable weight loss as that of a 750-calorie-per-day reduction, over a six-month period. While this may seem like novel information for most readers, for those athletes that rely on strength (how much "work" one can perform) and power (amount of work that can be performed per unit of time), the implications are the difference between being a champion or an "also ran." In the corporate world, similar dynamics are at play, and an equally sophisticated understanding of cost-cutting is warranted for companies that strive to be champions.

Consider the cautionary tale of a telco reducing its overhead support to its sales force. This enabled costs to be cut without affecting the numbers of front-line employees who actually made the sales. Costs fell as hoped, but the second-order effect was that frontline sales reps began undertaking support tasks (reports, order tracking, developing sales materials). In turn, they spent less time with customers which not only hurt revenues but also eroded their skills over time. Moreover, as sales reps were more expensive than back office staff, the cost per unit of staff work was now higher, and the quality of that work lower—the front-line lacked the same skills as the support staff that had been let go. While it intended to trim the fat, in the end the company lost valuable sales muscle. Fast-forward two years and the entire sales model was abandoned as the company found itself in crisis.

A similar lesson was learned by a retailer that cut costs as part of a corporate turnaround program. The retailer's strategy was changing from one of limiting market-entry risk, so locating stores where others had already proven successful, to one of being first to market in new geographies. At the same time, the cost-cutting workstream was busy reducing the number and pay of its real-estate professionals—in effect, sabotaging the institutional capability needed to deliver the new strategy.

Just as not all weight loss is good weight loss, leaders of overhead cost reduction need to ensure their efforts won't become the enemy of top-line growth.

GOOD INTENTIONS

 65%

of companies aim to reduce costs to gain competitive advantage

BAD HABITS

 74%

agree that their cost-cutting focuses on what's easy to measure vs. what's most needed

Mismatch between cost-cutting intentions and outcomes

"Less than one in five cost-cutters were subsequently able to put their companies back on a profitable growth track." –The Conference Board

Why is it important?
YOU OFTEN **LOSE FAR MORE TALENT** THAN YOU EXPECT

AFTER A LONG and arduous budget planning cycle, the CFO reveals to the senior team that next year's budget plan is still short by US$13 million. Everyone in the team has already dug deep in their own businesses, so it's not obvious how to close the gap. "I suggest we cut 1 percent of our overhead staff", says the CFO. "If we do so quickly, we'll be able to close the gap even after paying out on average six months of severance pay." It's a tough call as no one wants to let people go, but ultimately the team agrees it's the best option.

Sounds reasonable, right? Think again. This team unknowingly just torpedoed their budget, likely doubling the expense gap that will need to be closed in the coming year. No doubt the team realized that layoffs by their nature would dampen morale—in fact, 86 percent of CFOs agree that significant short-term cost reduction programs can be strongly detrmiental to staff morale.[15] What they failed to appreciate, however, is that research shows that layoffs targeting just 1 percent of the workforce precede, on average, a 31 percent increase in turnover.[16]

Let's run the numbers. The company is literally the Fortune 500 average: 50,000 employees, an attrition rate of 16 percent, paying an average salary of US$53,000.[17] The 31 percent increase in turnover means that, in addition to the 500 overhead staff that will be laid off, roughly another 2,500 employees, who otherwise would have stayed, will choose to leave. Research shows that a good estimate for the cost of replacing these employees (hiring, on-boarding, training, and lost productivity) is roughly 20 percent of an annual salary, which makes the cost of this attrition over US$26 million![18] It doesn't take an accountant to know that paying US$26 million to save US$13 million is a bad deal!

Astute readers will correctly point out that the 1 percent workforce reduction is an on-going saving, whereas the turnover costs are one-time expenses. While true, and in the course of many years there is a positive return, any near-term impact the company was looking for has clearly been sabotaged. Others will point out that not all turnover is bad. While true, the challenge is that, of those not directly targetted, you don't have control over who leaves, and high performers are at risk for multiple reasons: cost-cutting doesn't generate excitement about the company's future, meanwhile they have attractive opportunities elsewhere; their competitive nature makes them averse to being laid off themselves, so any fear of being next makes them want to control their destiny; they recognize that fewer people doesn't mean less work and the higher workload will likely disproportionately fall on them to pick up—with little or no additional reward; and so on.

The relationship between talent retention and overhead cost-reduction programs harkens back to the diet analogy. When trying to lose weight, most faced with getting a Big Mac or going to a salad bar would feel compelled to do the latter. Yet, by the time the bed of lettuce has bacon bits, deli meats, oily dressing, and blue cheese added, it can be double the calories of the fast-food option. Similarly, the attrition related to layoffs is the equivalent of those "hidden calories" and leaders must take it into account if they are to successfully reduce overheads.

"Layoffs targeting just 1% of the workforce precedes, on average, a 31% increase in turnover."
— Harvard Business Review

- **!** Want to control their own destiny
- **!** Severance and external opportunities
- **!** Frustration with lack of culture change
- **!** Additional workload without more reward
- **!** Lack of excitement about the company

Reasons high performers leave during cost reduction

What are the big ideas?
USE **SEVEN LEVERS**

AN EXPERT in overhead cost-reduction finds herself nominated by her company to serve on the board of her community's symphony orchestra. Before the first board meeting she wants to take in a performance. As she watches Schubert's "Unfinished Symphony," she takes notes to report back observations to the board. The notes are organized around the seven efficiency levers she applies at work:

DEMAND MANAGEMENT: Most listeners are unable to distinguish the rapid playing of sixteenth notes or semi-quavers. It is recommended that all notes be rounded up to the nearest eighth.

CONSOLIDATION AND CENTRALIZATION: No useful purpose is served by repeating with horns the same passage that has already been handled by the strings. By eliminating all such redundant passages the concert would have been reduced from two hours to about twenty minutes.

SMART SOURCING: If the above-mentioned changes were put in place, it would also be possible to use trainees and lower-grade musicians with no loss of quality.

LEAN MANAGEMENT AND PROCESS OPTIMIZATION: For considerable periods, the four oboe players had nothing to do. Their numbers should be reduced, and their work spread over the whole orchestra, thus eliminating peaks and valleys of activity.

TECHNOLOGY ENABLEMENT AND AUTOMATION: All twelve violins were playing identical notes with identical motions. The staff of this section should be cut drastically and the volume required obtained through electronic amplification.

ORGANIZATION STRUCTURE AND GOVERNANCE: The attendance of the conductor is unnecessary for public performances. The orchestra has obviously practiced and has the prior authorization from the conductor to play the symphony at a predetermined level of quality.

MINDSETS AND CAPABILITIES: A different mindset needs to be adopted by composers to take into account cost-containment principles. If Schubert had addressed these concerns, he would have been able to finish this symphony![19]

This is a light-hearted way to illustrate the seven levers we recommend leaders consider as part of zero-based overhead cost-reduction. A few practical examples of savings from each lever include: eliminating existing low-value reporting (demand management); creating shared service centers (consolidation and centralization); offshoring (smart sourcing); standardizing work (lean management and process optimization); enabling self-service of transactional activities (technology enablement and automation); optimizing spans and layers (organization structure and governance), and creating management rotation programs (mindsets and capabilities).

The absurdity of the "Unfinished Symphony" recommendations serve as a reminder that the levers have to be pulled in concert (pun intended!), and that they should all be considered in the context of how they support strategic objectives—solving only for costs will no doubt deliver catastrophic results!

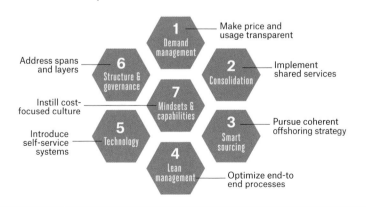

Example cost reduction actions by lever

What are the big ideas?
TAKE A **ZERO-BASED** APPROACH

YOU'RE IN the supermarket with the week's shopping list in hand. You head to the soup aisle to get the next item. Bingo! Campbell's soup is on sale for 79 cents. A sign above the display says "Limit 12 per customer." Now, how many cans do you buy? Believe it or not, there is research to answer this exact question, and on average seven cans are purchased. The research has also observed shoppers looking at the identical sale price in other stores, but with no purchase limit. How many cans do shoppers purchase on average in these situations? 3.3.[20] What's going on here?

Marketers in this case are taking advantage of what psychologists Daniel Kahneman and Amos Tversky identified in 1974 as the "anchoring heuristic." (A heuristic is essentially a mental shortcut or rule of thumb the brain uses to simplify complex problems in order to make decisions—also known as a cognitive bias, which we discussed in further detail in our chapter on decision-making). The anchoring rule of thumb relies too heavily on the first piece of information offered (the "anchor") in making decisions, regardless of the legitimacy of the anchor. In our supermarket example, shoppers' brains exposed to the purchase limit anchored on 12 and adjusted downward.

Now let's think about the traditional approach to cost-cutting: department managers start with their existing budget (the "anchor") and are expected to look for cost reductions against that historical baseline. What if the "anchor" were replaced by zero? No cost is taken as a given—instead, every cost has to be justified by how it contributes to delivering against the company's strategy and in the forward-looking market context in which the company operates. Research indicates that doing so finds savings above and beyond traditional approaches of, on average, 25 percent.[21]

This is a more arduous process than traditional overhead reduction approaches in that every line item of the budget is scrutinized, alternatives explored, and every dollar justified for approval, not just the changes proposed against the baseline. The benefits, however, aren't just in the incremental savings. A zero-based approach also breaks the mentality of entitlement around having a large budget. Further, it explicitly ensures spend is directed towards strategic objectives and functional missions—thereby guarding against cutting in areas that shouldn't be cut. Its comprehensiveness also makes sure there is no "squeezing of the balloon" where costs in one area are reduced but then are incurred in other areas to compensate for the change. Finally, advances in technology and analytics enable today's application of a zero-based approach to be far less burdensome than in previous eras.

In a fast-changing world, the future looks very different from the past. Your cost base should too. Just as many families can eliminate their home telephones and cable TV subscriptions in a world of mobile phone ubiquity and on-line entertainment options, so too can opportunities be found to reduce duplicative or "nice-to-have" spend via a zero-based approach.

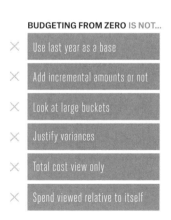

BUDGETING FROM ZERO IS...	BUDGETING FROM ZERO IS NOT...
✓ Start from zero, with a target	✗ Use last year as a base
✓ Build bottom-up	✗ Add incremental amounts or not
✓ Granular level of detail	✗ Look at large buckets
✓ Justify every line item	✗ Justify variances
✓ Price and volume driver view	✗ Total cost view only
✓ All spend linked to KPIs	✗ Spend viewed relative to itself

Key features of a zero-based approach

What are the big ideas?
SOLVE FOR SMART,
NOT SIMPLE

ONE OF the most frequently employed approaches to reduce overhead costs is that of "spans and layers," where "spans" refers to the number of employees that a manager can effectively control and "layers" denotes the different levels of hierarchy. Common management wisdom is that companies should "flatten" (also known as "delayering") by increasing spans and reducing layers. The promise is that this approach will not only reduce costs, but also increase accountability, empowerment, customer focus, and market responsiveness.

If you look up what the optimum spans and layers are, most literature will tell you that spans of seven and eight layers are the magic numbers to aim for.[22] Sounds promising, right? Think again. To use a golf analogy, this is like a golf instructor telling you, "The average distance a pro golfer hits the ball is ninety meters on any given hole. Use a pitching wedge (the club that hits the ball roughly ninety meters) for every shot." We've seen countless delayering programs, that cascade 7x8 targets through an organization, get bogged down or abandoned once leaders realize that they are being asked to do the managerial equivalent of using a pitching wedge on a putting green. Research by Harvard Business School Professor, Julie Wulf, confirms, "Flattening can lead to exactly the opposite effects from [those] it promises." She points out that after delayering, most leaders end up spending more time on internal (not customer or market-related) issues. And decision-making becomes more, not less, command and control.[23]

A smarter, even if not as simple, approach to spans and layers is to incorporate the idea of "managerial archetypes" into the process—explicitly acknowledging that spans of control should differ based on the type of role needed. For example, in roles where there is no standard work and direct reports perform unique tasks that need apprenticeship to complete, the ideal span of control is 3–5 (this is what we call a "Player-coach" role—perhaps the putter in our golf analogy). Contrast this to a role where work is completely standardized and intervention is required only for exceptions; here the ideal span of control is greater than 15 (this is what we call a "coordinator" role—or the driver in our golf analogy). Other roles leaders can play are "coach" (6–7 is ideal), "supervisor" (8–10 is appropriate), and "facilitator" (11–15 is best).

Using this more sophisticated approach, spans become fit for purpose, and the resulting layers are appropriate. In addition, discussions on the right archetype for each role help align leadership expectations, uncover the root causes of why things are unbalanced to begin with, and generate further cost-reduction ideas. Done smartly versus simply, spans and layers can powerfully reduce an organization's overhead "handicap."

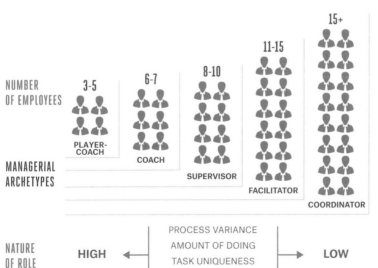

Managerial archetypes and their drivers

How do I make it happen?
FOLLOW A **FIVE-STEP PROCESS** TO REDUCE OVERHEAD COSTS

AN AUSTRALIAN industrial packaging manufacturer was facing new challenges. After years of being one of a few players in a relatively protected market, regulations had changed and international competitors were pouring in. Asian companies with far lower cost bases were aggressively pricing, driving margins down significantly. During their recent strategy review, the senior team agreed they wouldn't try and compete on cost, but instead differentiate through valued-added features and services. At the same time, they knew every penny mattered now more than ever. They also recognized that too little discipline had existed regarding overhead costs, and attacking these with rigor could make a significant difference to their ability to compete—both from a pricing and an agility standpoint.

1. Aspire

THE FIRST order of business was to align on the objectives. To aid this process, the company's strategy team was asked to pull together a fact base that included the overall costs by area, internal and external best-practice benchmarks, competitive intelligence, and the implications of the company's strategy for its overhead support structure. The data showed the opportunity was even bigger than imagined. As a result of their paternalistic culture, they had long opted to move lower performers into functional roles instead of moving them on. Over time, significant redundancy had to be built in to work around these lower performers. And, as the company grew, span-breaking positions were added which attracted their own overhead structure, increasing cost and complexity.

Informed by the facts, the senior team set a bold target of a 50 percent reduction in overhead costs. The CEO captured its spirit in saying, "This isn't about finding ways to cut 50 percent of what we have today; it's determining what we need for the future and spending up to 50 percent of today to make it happen." The targets applied to all overhead functions, including all of the staff in the corporate headquarters, regions, and local sites, and including everyone who supported functional activities—whether or not they were technically on that support function's books. Guiding principles were also set to ensure muscle was protected and built where needed based on the strategy, not just blanket cost reduction.

Aspire
Where do we want to go?

Cost objectives: Define context, scope, cost reductions, and business improvement targets

Strategic objectives: Distill strategic requirements for growth, operations, and culture

Strengths and pain points: Understand key performance drivers, capabilities, and talent needed for future; identify what is not working well

Design criteria: Synthesize all of the above into specific sources of value and criteria to guide design

2. Assess

A WORKING TEAM was formed, led by one of the company's high performers, to work with each function to pull together detailed cost baselines, articulate their mission and role in support of the new strategy, define their 3–5 most important "value streams" (end-to-end processes that deliver the most important outcomes to support the business), and identify the related measures of successful delivery. All of the data was then assessed against internal and external benchmarks to help prioritize where to focus.

Once every function had developed their baselines, the full cross-functional picture was reviewed and a three-step process to capture the value developed. The first step would be to make any overall organization structure changes. Second, each function's value streams were radically redesigned within the new structure—cutting out unnecessary steps and automating as many areas as possible. Finally, spans and layers within the redesigned organization were optimized, ensuring they were in keeping with fit-for-purpose principles.

Assess
How ready are we to go there?

Baseline: Develop an accurate baseline for the organization's size, shape, cost, key capabilities, and talent needs

Benchmarks: Assess current metrics against best practices

Prioritization: Understand key activities, what adds value, and what can be removed

3. Architect

DURING THE FIRST STEP, the regional layer of support was removed altogether (with a few exceptions for legal and risk purposes). It was clear that what had previously been put in place as a span-breaker had grown into cumbersome, bureaucratic mini-empires. Strategic, control, and transactional activities were pushed to the center (housed in shared services and centers of excellence). Activities important to customer responsiveness or day-to-day execution were pushed to the local level. Rules of the road for the new structure were articulated, including items such as the role of the center being to optimize for the company as a whole (local sites needed to accept that this might not optimize for them) and that a common operating model would be adopted across the functions (e.g. all functions have a business partner "at the table" with site leadership, even though that partner supports multiple sites).

A "zero-based" approach was then applied to determine how best to deliver the core value streams in each function. In some areas the solution was to outsource many of the related activities (e.g. payroll processing), and in others the application of lean principles, technology, and demand-management methods led to end-to-end expense reductions of up to 80 percent. Once the value streams were redesigned, spans and layers within each function were optimized. In transaction-related areas, leaders played a coordinator role and therefore were held to a standard of a large span of control, whereas in the strategy area a player/ coach role was needed, and therefore a low span of control was expected. At the end of the three steps the overall cost base of the new model was determined—and was found to be only 30 percent that of the existing model. Needless to say, senior leadership gave the green light to move to the next stage of implementation planning.

Architect
What do we need to do to get there?

Zero-based structural design: Clean-sheet what the optimal design would be within any "hard" constraints; compare clean sheet against baseline to identify opportunities

Processes: Redesign, develop, and pressure-test end-to-end processes, ensuring activities and number of people involved are streamlined

Zero-based budgets: Use re-organization as a trigger to budget from zero in both personnel and non-personnel costs

4. Act

THE WORK was implemented in the IT, Finance, and HR teams first, so that they could operate more efficiently to support the other functions with changes to their budgets, role and reporting lines, and tools and systems. This also meant that the company could provide a longer glide path out of the organization: those being laid off could apply to be in a temporary pool of contract workers that would help get work done during the transition. Implementation staging also took into account the magnitude of change that would be experienced at the local level, to ensure day-to-day delivery of the business or major milestones (e.g. equipment changeovers, product introductions) wouldn't be put at risk.

A comprehensive communications plan was also put together taking into account the needs of both internal and external stakeholders. Everything from the compelling reasons why the changes had to be made, what the changes would be and when, and how the new model was expected to work, were mapped out to take employees on a journey from awareness to understanding to commitment and capability to work in the new model. Care was taken to ensure the process was fair and thoughtful, so that employees knew what they would experience and when, in particular in relation to the layoffs. Care was also taken to ensure high performers had individualized outreach to let them know they were valued, to answer any questions, and get feedback.

Act
How do we manage the journey?

Roll-out plan: Develop plan to cascade detailed design including the day 1 launch, roadmap, and team charters for each initiative

Training and communications plan: Develop external and internal communications and training plans by stakeholder, ensuring they address the "why" for all employees

Governance model: Ensure sponsorship, change support, metrics, and tracking mechanisms are in place

5. Advance

DURING IMPLEMENTATION of the new model, a "war room" was used to keep tabs on progress. Initially the main metrics measured related to hitting milestones, employee morale, talent retention, and business continuity. As they were developed, delivery against "service level agreements" (a.k.a. SLAs—agreements between the businesses and functions in relation to the cost, quality, and service levels to be delivered for each value stream), were also measured. These proved that not only was the overhead structure substantially less expensive, but it was delivering at higher levels in many areas than the previous one.

As implementation challenges emerged, they were generally dealt with successfully by going back to the rules of the road that everyone had bought into early in the process. The central working team stayed together running the war room, ensuring there was a place to raise and resolve concerns until implementation was complete. The first time the planning and budget cycle came around was another test, as functional leaders found it challenging not to fall into old habits of empire-building and being soft on performance management. The newly instituted zero-based budgeting process that required every line item to be justified based on the business strategy (vs. looking at variances from the previous year) was instrumental to helping new habits form, even if less comfortable than the old way.

Advance
How do we keep moving forward?

Execution monitoring: Monitor against key milestones and operational and financial metrics

Talent management: Take steps to retain top talent with both short-term and long-term incentives

Employee engagement: Ensure employees feel supported and their concerns are addressed

Business continuity: Safeguard key processes, customer servicing, and performance reporting

A YEAR AFTER they had begun implementation, the new structure was in place and working. While it had been hard to exit staff, the process was seen by all as having been fair—treating those affected with dignity and respect and supporting them in finding roles outside. Furthermore, the senior team had significantly more freedom to win in the marketplace with the lower costs and increased agility. One thing that surprised the team was the extent to which functional leaders lower down in the organization took pride in their company being considered "best-practice" in expense management, so much so that many even talked with their teams about what the "next practice" could be that would further lead the industry.

OVERHEAD COST REDUCTION:
AT A GLANCE

 WHY IS IT IMPORTANT?

- Value creating companies keep costs under control.

- Done poorly, it sabotages future growth.

- You often lose far more talent than you plan.

 WHAT ARE THE BIG IDEAS?

- Use seven levers.

- Take a zero-based approach.

- Solve for smart, not simple.

 HOW DO I MAKE IT HAPPEN?

- Follow a five-step process to reduce overhead costs.

  Most commonly neglected action in each step:

  Aspire: Balance growth, culture, and cost objectives.

  Assess: Fully understand go forward capabilities needed.

  Architect: Design early warning triggers for cost build back.

  Act: Develop robust stakeholder communications plans.

  Advance: Take proactive steps to engage and retain talent.

III. CULTURE AND CHANGE

8

How do I make culture a competitive advantage?

Culture:
A TIMELESS TOPIC

EVERY YEAR there are thousands of forest fires, yet only a few turn into the roaring blazes that make the headlines. Why? Because in most circumstances the physical environment precludes that from happening—ample rainfall keeps wooded areas moist, well-equipped fire departments stand ready, wind and weather patterns can be predicted, etc. Every year in every organization there are thousands of good ideas and best practices surfaced, yet very few ever reap game-changing benefits from these spreading like wildfire. Why? Because the work environment, a.k.a. the culture, precludes that from happening via bureaucracy, resistance to change, silos, hierarchical behavior, etc.

What exactly is culture? At the observable level, it's the patterns of shared behavior and practices that are visible in an organization, or more simply said, "The way things get done around here." Look more deeply, however, and one can find the shared perceptions, attitudes, beliefs, and values that are "beneath the surface;" a bit like an iceberg, they are not observable but have great significance These are the lens through which one's past and present are interpreted to inform how best to survive and thrive into the future.

Look at ancient history, be it to the Persians, Romans, or Egyptians, and you will find cultural underpinnings contribute to both the rise and fall of great empires. Fast-forward to the eighteenth century, with the advent of modern economic theory, and the link between culture and performance was formalized: Adam Smith's *Theory of*

Moral Sentiments dealt with many aspects of what we would now call culture. In the nineteenth century, economists such as John Stuart Mill reinforced the notion that cultural constraints on individuals can have a stronger impact on them than personal financial gain. In the early twentieth century, German social scientist Max Weber offered more specific insights into how culture can affect economic impact—arguing that the Protestant work ethic inculcated the virtues needed for maximum productivity and explained the vast differences in output between countries endowed with similar resources.[1] Now it's well accepted that, as Harvard historian David Landes said, "If we learn anything from the history of economic development, it is that culture makes all the difference".[2]

Companies consist of groups of people working together. Where there are people working together there is a culture, whether a leader chooses to influence it or not. But this is soft stuff—how much does it really matter versus the many other levers a leader has to drive performance? And are there genuinely reliable tools available to leaders to shape the culture? Read on to find out...

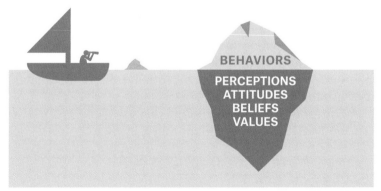

Culture is the way things get done around here...and why

Why is it important?

CULTURE **DRIVES** PERFORMANCE

MOST LEADERS are squeamish about approaching the topic of culture. Some see it as better left to organizational psychologists. Others simply don't know how to make it happen. And still others simply don't believe it can be meaningfully influenced in their tenures. As such, they give the topic lip service, but seldom take it as seriously as more concrete business operational and strategic performance levers.

Unfortunately, these leaders are putting their heads well and truly in the sand. Whether one looks at Kotter & Heskett's landmark eleven-year study that showed companies with strong cultures had cumulative annual growth rates in revenues, stock price, and net income that far outpaced those with weak cultures,[3] or fifteen years of McKinsey & Company research that shows companies with strong performance cultures achieve three times higher total return to shareholders (TRS) than those that don't,[4] the evidence that culture is a profound driver of business performance is incontrovertible.

The facts are seldom enough to sway leaders, however, so we won't dwell on them here. Research from Yale Professor Dan Kahan shows that the more quantitative a person is (i.e. most business leaders) the more likely it is that they will entrench into even more wrong views when confronted with data that proves their current outlook to be wrong (for more on this phenomenon see our chapter on decision-making)![5]

Perhaps a more helpful way to illustrate the link between culture and performance is Gary Hamel and C. K. Prahalad's apocryphal story of four monkeys:[6]

Four monkeys are sitting in a cage with a bunch of bananas hanging from the roof, accessible by a set of steps. Whenever the monkeys try to climb the steps to get to the bananas, they are blocked by a blast of cold water. After a few days, the monkeys give up. Researchers then remove the water hose and replace one of the original monkeys with a new one. Seeing the bananas, it starts up the steps. What happens? The other monkeys, being social creatures, pull it down before it gets blasted with water. This happens again and again until pretty soon the new monkey doesn't bother to go for the bananas either. Over the next few weeks, the researchers remove the rest of the original monkeys one at a time and replace them with new monkeys who've never seen the jet of water. Even though there's no longer anything to stop the monkeys from reaching the bananas, each new monkey is always pulled down by the others. By the end of the experiment, not a single monkey has ever seen a jet of water, but none of them tries to climb the steps. They've all learned the unwritten rule that "You don't grab the bananas around here."

The notion that otherwise natural steps to improve business performance may be blocked by "the way things get done around here" strikes a chord with most leaders.

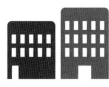

Performance of organizations that focus on culture versus their peers

Across Industries

Companies with strong cultures, regardless of industry, outperform the stock market by

3X

Across Companies

Companies that focus on culture show a

9%

increase in EBITA after one year

Within Companies

Culture explains up to

50%

of performance variation across units

Why is it important?

IT'S **HARD TO COPY**

NETFLIX'S CULTURAL MANIFESTO, "Netflix Culture: Freedom & Responsibility",[7] has been read and admired by over 15 million leaders around the world. Yet how many of those leaders created a similar "no formal process" culture in their organizations? Spotify's "Engineering culture" video has experienced similar viral appeal, but how many companies have successfully adopted their agile approaches at scale? We suspect very few—certainly we haven't run across them in our work on culture.

This is not dissimilar to why Toyota's lean production system has been one of the most written about and studied approaches to efficient manufacturing for the last thirty years, yet few companies looking to replicate Toyota's approach have reaped the rewards they've sought. Or why, despite Southwest Airline's model for low-cost air travel having been the subject of case study after case study, most low-cost airlines still struggle to survive for more than a few years. The same can be said for how Ritz Carlton sets standards in customer service, how Proctor & Gamble manages its brands, how General Electric replicates its business model across multiple industries, and many others.

It's also why when companies hire employees from others famous for their performance cultures, they are often disappointed with the outcomes. Take, for example, J. C. Penney's poaching of Apple's Head of Retail Operations, Ron Johnson, to be their CEO. His seventeen-month stint trying to replicate Apple's formula at Penney's resulted in a US$4bn loss in revenues and a plummeting stock price.[8]

The reason? Culture is inherently hard to copy. Just like riding a bike, it cannot be read about or simply observed to be understood; it has to be experienced. Contrast this to other assets. Given enough time and money, competitors can reverse-engineer your processes, acquire similar (if not better) physical assets, and copy your strategy. What's more, the time and money required to do so will only continue to compress with the forces of globalization, the instant and often costless availability of information, the increased mobility of talent, and ever more readily available capital.

Nearly fifty years after management guru Peter Drucker is said to have stated, "Culture eats strategy for breakfast"[9], there is a strong case for culture dining on strategy for lunch and dinner as well! Successful business leaders agree. In the words of Warren Buffett, CEO of Berkshire Hathaway and one of the world's most successful investors, "Our final advantage is the hard-to-duplicate culture that permeates Berkshire. And in businesses, culture counts."[10]

Toyota	**Continuous improvement**	"The 'Toyota way' is first and foremost about company culture." *Harvard Business Review*
SOUTHWEST.COM	**Customer experience**	"Competitors can buy tangible assets, but they can't buy culture." *Herb Kelleher, former CEO, Southwest Airlines*
Google	**Innovation**	"Nurturing a culture that allows for innovation is key to Google's 'secret sauce'." *Larry Page, CEO, Google*

Iconic examples of cultural competitive advantage

Why is it important?
UNDER-MANAGED, IT
CAN BE YOUR UNDOING

THE QUESTION "Does your organization's culture help or hinder its performance?" was posed at the beginning of this chapter. The facts, unfortunately, suggest that the answer for many leaders is the latter.

Most leaders are aware of the dismal statistic that only one in three change programs succeed. Fewer realize that the reason, in the vast majority of cases, is cultural.[11] More insidious, however, is that cultural dysfunctions don't just keep a company from capturing upsides, they can ultimately threaten an organization's very existence.

An iconic example of culture fail is Enron, whose obsessive short-term-return culture caused it to develop increasingly complex off-balance-sheet financing systems that drove it to Chapter 11 bankruptcy in 2001. In the hope of ensuring companies avoided such spectacular collapses in the future, regulators and law makers put in place significant financial and accounting reforms. Culture trumped policies and procedures, however, when the world again witnessed similar collapses during the 2008 financial crisis as companies such as Lehman Brothers became intoxicated with short-term returns.[12]

Further examples abound. In the case of Barclays Libor-rigging scandal, the Salz Review determined "cultural shortcomings" to be the root cause.[13] In the case of General Motor's filing for bankruptcy in 2009, GM's core problem was described as "its corporate and workplace culture."[14] Volkswagen's culture or tolerance for rule-breaking is widely regarded as having led to its recent "Dieselgate" scandal.[15] In the case of BP, and its 2010 Deepwater Horizon catastrophe, the worst environmental disaster the region had ever seen was driven by dysfunction in the company's safety and risk culture.[16]

It's recently come into vogue in management literature to think about toxic cultures as akin to having "dirty aquarium water."[17] If not tended to, ultimately it proves fatal. Like aquarium water, however, culture can be changed—though it takes a concerted effort. Take IBM, whose culture of arrogance and insularity led it to the brink. In the words of Lou Gerstner, the former CEO who turned the company around, "Fixing culture is the most critical—and the most difficult—part of a corporate transformation."[18]

With that in mind, let's turn to the big ideas that will enable you to make any needed culture change happen in your organization...

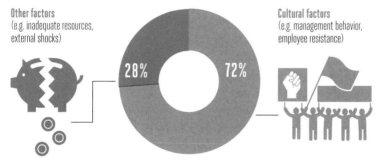

Other factors
(e.g. inadequate resources,
external shocks)

Cultural factors
(e.g. management behavior,
employee resistance)

28%   72%

*Reasons change
programs fail*

What are the big ideas?

FOCUS ON MORE THAN EMPLOYEE ENGAGEMENT

"HOW DO YOU MEASURE CULTURE?" we often ask senior leaders. "We conduct an annual engagement survey" is the most common answer we hear. WRONG ANSWER. The proponents of employee engagement surveys have convinced leaders that higher employee engagement means better business results. It's not that they're lying—they've got the numbers to back it up—it's that, unbeknownst to many proponents, they simply aren't providing the whole truth.

We've reviewed over 900 top-tier academic studies to distill the full set of cultural measures empirically proven to drive improved performance.[19] The results group into nine elements:

DIRECTION: A clear sense of where the organization is headed and how it will get there that is meaningful to all employees.

LEADERSHIP: The extent to which leaders inspire actions by others.

WORK ENVIRONMENT: The quality of interactions within and across organizational units.

ACCOUNTABILITY: The extent to which individuals understand what is expected of them, have sufficient authority to carry it out, and take responsibility for delivering results.

COORDINATION AND CONTROL: The ability to evaluate organizational performance and risk, and to work together to address issues and opportunities as they arise.

CAPABILITIES: The presence of institutional skills and talent required to execute strategy and create competitive advantage.

MOTIVATION: The presence of enthusiasm that drives employees to put in extraordinary effort to deliver results.

EXTERNAL ORIENTATION: The quality of engagement with customers, suppliers, partners, and other external stakeholders to drive value.

INNOVATION AND LEARNING: The quality and flow of new ideas and the organization's ability to adapt and shape itself as needed.

This is the set of measures that matter. But it's not just breadth that engagement surveys miss the mark on, it's also depth. If the above are the organizational equivalent to the vital signs of human health—heart rate, blood pressure, weight, etc.—you'd never be satisfied with a doctor's report that simply says "you're at high risk of a heart attack" if it didn't also indicate what you can practically do in order to reduce your risk. Similarly, leaders need not just to assess the outcomes they are getting from their culture, but also the practices. For example, if a measurement tool indicates there is low accountability, it should also tell you which management practices you should improve to get more: is it improving role clarity, creating stronger performance contracts, increasing consequence management, and/or fostering more personal ownership? Bottom line: measure the nine outcomes that matter most and the practices that drive them, not just engagement.

Elements of culture
that matter most
to performance

What are the big ideas?
SHIFT **UNDERLYING MINDSETS** THAT DRIVE BEHAVIORS

WE'VE TALKED about the importance of measuring cultural outcomes and the management practices that drive them. That's not the whole story, however. Changing management practices seldom in and of itself creates the magnitude and speed of culture change that leaders aspire to. After all, organizations don't change, people do.

Consider the "monkeys in the cage" story we shared earlier. The outcome was that the monkeys didn't climb the ladder. The practice that initially caused that outcome—the blast of water that knocked the monkeys off the ladder—had been changed. Behaviors stayed the same, however, because the mindset that had been ingrained by the previous practice remained: "We don't grab the bananas around here."

Let's make this real. Consider a bank looking to grow its sales. First, it looked at what its top sales people were doing differently from the others and found they had a greater knowledge of the product set and spent more time profiling customers to match products with customer needs. Knowing this, the bank's leaders then created a change program aimed at giving the average salespeople more product knowledge, and providing them with tools and incentives to ask more profiling questions. The program was rolled out with great fanfare, effort, and cost...and sales barely improved.

Why? Good question—and one the bank should have asked in the following way: why, while working in the same organizational system, do some sales people choose to learn more about the products and spend more time profiling customers? We helped the bank answer this question, and it came down to two underlying mindsets: the average sales people believed, "My job is to give the customer what they want" whereas the high performers believed "My job is to help my customer understand what they really need." Also, average performers held to the golden rule, "Treat the customer the way I want to be treated" vs. the platinum rule, "Treat the customer the way they want to be treated."

The average sales people hadn't been aware of the fundamental assumptions they had been making, or that there were alternate ones that could enable them to better serve customers. When these were called out and people were offered a choice as to what to believe, the change was almost instantaneous. Tools and information that had previously been pushed unsuccessfully onto the workforce were now proactively pulled for and put into practice, and this led to a 43 percent increase in cross sell in the subsequent year.

Uncovering mindsets isn't as hard as one may think—there are a number of interview, card-sort, and text-analysis tools that can get to root causes quickly. When leaders put these methods into practice, the truth of the famous statement often attributed to Albert Einstein, "We cannot solve today's problems with the same level of thinking that created them"[20] is fully understood.

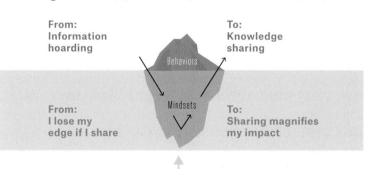

Ⓐ To shift this behavior, leaders typically install large knowledge-management systems...

Ⓑ ...and then are disappointed that such systems are never used in a meaningful way...

From:
Information
hoarding

To:
Knowledge
sharing

Behaviors

From:
I lose my
edge if I share

Mindsets

To:
Sharing magnifies
my impact

Ⓒ ...because mindsets did not shift (had the right mindsets been in place, new systems would never have been needed).

The peril of ignoring the power of mindsets: Knowledge sharing example

What are the big ideas?
USE **FOUR HIGH-IMPACT** **LEVERS** TO GET THE JOB DONE

THUS FAR we've talked about how to measure culture and the importance of honing in on the critical management practice changes and underlying mindset shifts that will unlock performance. But what can you actually *do* to shift the culture?

By way of illustration, let's assume you are one of the vast majority of people who believe "skydiving isn't worth the risk." Let's say we want to shift your mindset to believe that it is. What if we put in place the following?

A COMPELLING STORY: We will donate US$1 million to the charity of your choice for every jump you do, and show you reliable data that shows the chances of being injured are far less than driving to work each day.

REINFORCING MECHANISMS: Your bonus will be increased ten-fold this year if you do it, and will be withheld if you don't; and we've ensured you will have world-class safety equipment, including an automatic back-up chute.

CONFIDENCE AND SKILLS: A world champion skydiver will give you in-depth lessons before you jump, (including a number of simulations) and ease any underlying fears you may have.

ROLE MODELING: Your boss, two of your colleagues, your immediate family, and your closest friends will do it with you. What's more, others close to you have already done it—and loved it!

Would you now be willing to jump out of a perfectly good airplane? The last hundred years of behavioral and cognitive psychology would say that you would be far more likely to. Social science tells us that these are the four levers which leaders can use to shift mindsets and behaviors.

Many leaders wonder which lever is most important. While the research suggests there is some variation, experience is clear that they all matter. Culture efforts not thoughtfully engineered on all four levers can cause more harm than good. Imagine pursuing a cost-conscious culture while executives are flying around to cushy offsite meetings in corporate jets, or pushing for collaboration when incentives reinforce putting silos first, or asking the front line to have a stronger risk culture without giving them the training needed to enable them to do so. In these cases, nothing is achieved other than increased frustration and cynicism that fuel resistance to future change.

Successful culture change efforts aren't pursued in parallel with other business improvement efforts, but are integrated fully with them. The practical manifestation of this is often that any business case asking for investment dollars has to explicitly specify the cultural impact it will have using each of the four levers.

When a concentrated effort is made on all four and the primary delivery vehicle is through business improvement efforts, impact can happen more quickly than most leaders expect. We've seen large companies move from bottom- to top-quartile cultural effectiveness within eighteen months, then sustain and improve on those results.[21]

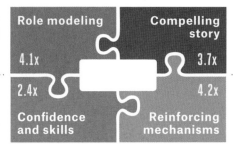

- Leadership actions
- Top team dynamics
- Influence leaders

Role modeling 4.1x

Compelling story 3.7x

- Change story
- Two-way communications
- Language, rituals

- Learning journeys
- Personal insights
- Refresh talent pool

2.4x **Confidence and skills**

4.2x **Reinforcing mechanisms**

- Incentives
- Structure
- Process and systems

Four influence levers and how much they increase the probability of success in shifting culture

Many of these elements are described in more detail in previous chapters.

How do I make it happen?

FOLLOW A **FIVE-STEP PROCESS** TO INFLUENCE CULTURE CHANGE

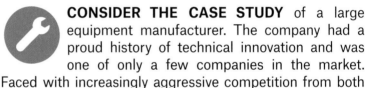

CONSIDER THE CASE STUDY of a large equipment manufacturer. The company had a proud history of technical innovation and was one of only a few companies in the market. Faced with increasingly aggressive competition from both traditional and non-traditional players and a changing market place, they found themselves slipping behind other large industrials both in performance and in the battle for capital, talent, and influence. As they aspired to get back on top, they recognized their largely bureaucratic and complacent culture would be a significant inhibitor, and saw potential for culture change not only to be a performance accelerator, but a hard-to-copy competitive advantage for the company.

1. Aspire

First, the company set out to fully understand their current state to uncover the highest leverage points to intervene. It started by conducting the Organization Health Index (OHI) survey with all of its 9,000 managers (The OHI measures the nine elements of culture described in this chapter, both at the level of outcomes and practices). The results were hardly surprising—benchmarks against both the global OHI database and their industrial peers indicated their performance culture was in the third quartile. While they still made great products, they made it far harder to do so than it could or should be.

Using the OHI's predictive analytics engine, the survey results were analyzed to hone in on the critical management practices that would make the biggest difference in improving the culture and thereby improving performance. In their case, the top three most in need of an overhaul were: capturing external ideas, role clarity, and continuous improvement.

In the past, the approach to the engagement surveys called for every leader to look at their own data and determine for themselves what was important. However, if the culture was going to change, the company had to collectively focus on the same priorities so the senior team agreed to work together on these areas.

Aspire
Where do we want to go?

Shared language: Choose a culture model and vocabulary to work with to take the topic from abstraction to specifics

Baseline: Use quantitative and qualitative benchmarks to understand your starting point on outcomes and practices related to the nine dimensions that matter to performance

Strategic requirements: Focus on the cultural elements that will make the biggest difference to future business performance

2. Assess

Over fifty mindset and behavior interviews and focus groups were then conducted to understand why smart, hardworking, well-intentioned leaders weren't already doing these things well (and what was different about the few that were). Three core mindsets were discovered to be at the heart of the matter:

Their history of success with specialized products had led to a mindset of "we are peerless," which created myopic industry frame reference, an under-estimation of competitors (in particular from non-traditional arenas), and over-confidence.

Their engineering-centric workforce had developed a mindset of "fix problems with process" which led over time to a proliferation of processes and approvals that made it nearly impossible for people to know who could make a final decision on what.

Their proud history of step-change innovation led to a mindset that "we have to take giant leaps forward" which led to the churn of net new designs, ignoring the significant performance potential efficiencies of re-use and standardization.

Assess
How ready are we to go there?

Strengths and weaknesses: Identify the strengths you want to maintain and how they can be used to address weaknesses

Root-cause mindsets: Understand the mindsets that explain why employees behave the way they do and consider how these can be reframed

Engagement model: Determine how and when to engage the organization in the process (top team, broad leadership coalition, change agents, all employees)

3. Architect

In order to improve the practices that mattered most and shift the underlying mindsets, a robust plan was created against the four change levers. Efforts were sequenced and governance and measures were decided upon, to ensure it could be managed effectively. The full extent of the program could fill many pages, but some highlights of the plan included:

ROLE-MODELING: The senior team received 360-feedback related to their personal and team behaviors in relation to the target practices and mindset shifts, and a group of thirty change leaders were chosen from the senior ranks.

STORY-TELLING: A powerful change story was crafted describing why, why now, what, how, and who. A plan was created not just to tell the story, but to ensure everyone in the organization engaged with what it meant for them and their teams.

REINFORCING MECHANISMS: A SWAT-team approach was created to swiftly identify and fix where decision-rights were unclear in high-value areas. Targets were reframed vs. industrial peers, not just in absolute terms. Incentives were adjusted to reflect the importance of incremental gains vs. moon-shot innovation.

SKILL- AND CONFIDENCE-BUILDING: Plans were made to overhaul the company's leadership curriculum to drive the desired culture, in addition to looking for outside talent from leading industrials who would bring continuous improvement expertise.

Architect
What do we need to do to get there?

Role modeling: Determine a clear plan of action for the CEO, top team, and influence leaders

Story telling: Create a powerful change story, set of language markers, and overall communications plan

Formal mechanisms: Determine required adjustments to structures, processes, systems, and incentives

Skill building: Create a plan for each employee segment using field-and-forum approaches and introducing new talent as needed

4. Act

The plan was launched at a top-300 offsite where a broad group of leaders were exposed to both the Aspire and Assess findings, as well as the draft plan put together in the Architect phase. The session was led by the senior team, with the change leaders also playing a prominent role, and all participants were empowered to offer refinements to the plan. The focus of the session was on "what does this mean for me and my area?" and the findings were extremely well received, with many leaders indicating "Finally, we're talking about the real stuff that holds us back!"

The offsite kicked off an interactive cascade that flowed through the entire organization over the next two months—centering on a full-day interactive session that crisply articulated the change story and prompted dialogue around: "How can the cultural focus areas help us unlock further performance?"; "What will we do (using the four levers available) to capture the value?"; "How will we hold ourselves accountable?" The sessions also included 360-feedback related to the target culture so that participants could reflect on and publically commit to "What change will I make in myself that will make the biggest difference to the culture change we aspire to?"

Meanwhile, pilot initiatives that integrated culture change and performance improvement were undertaken in the product development and supply chain functions. The approach was then replicated for other major business initiatives. Progress was monitored regularly and efforts adjusted as needed, and company communications consistently reinforced expectations and pointed towards successes and learnings.

Act
How do we manage the journey?

Business initiative engineering: Ensure every major business initiative is engineered to reflect the desired culture in the way it's run

Making it personal: Ensure a critical mass of leaders form a deep personal commitment to make culture change happen

Support infrastructure: Use a PMO to monitor and manage the journey from awareness to commitment to institutionalization

Viral communications: Foster bottom-up development of ideas and best-practice sharing

5. Advance

OVER TIME new rituals took hold—one of which was the use of a green and yellow card used to call out good and bad behaviors on the spot (analogous to giving a "yellow card" in the game of soccer). On the yellow side were the "from" mindsets: "We are peerless," "Fix problems with process," and "Take giant leaps." On the green side were the "to" mindsets: "We are competitive," "Prevent problems through people," "Improve with every stride."

In addition, those joining the organization were indoctrinated into the desired culture. This was reinforced in everything from recruiting, on-boarding, and training, to promotion and reward criteria, and as such new entrants were seen as playing a vital role in "holding up the mirror" to whether or not the change was really happening.

To gauge progress the company considered a traditional "pulse" survey. The survey had ten questions. The first six were designed to get a read on the absolute (how much is there?) and relative (how much change have you experienced?) progress being made on the three target management practices. The final four asked employees the extent to which they saw each of the four levers being used to influence the desired mindset shifts. In the end, however, they used a "live" approach—using the full set of OHI questions deployed across a broad set of employees receiving only one of the questions on a rotating basis. This meant they had a continuous pulse on the culture while minimizing the survey burden.

Advance
How do we keep moving forward?

Rituals: Embed culture-reinforcing actions into day-to-day routines and communications mechanisms

Talent management: Infuse the desired culture into talent-management processes (e.g. recruiting, onboarding, development, promotion criteria, evaluation, recognition, and celebration)

Ongoing monitoring: Continue to rigorously measure culture using qualitative and quantitative metrics

TWO YEARS AFTER they had embarked on their journey, the company re-administered the Organization Health Index (OHI) survey across all of its 9,000 managers. As had been hoped, the difference was profound—against both the global OHI database and their industrial peers they were now in the top quartile. This was hardly unexpected, however, given the tone of the company had palpably shifted: employees took pride in the continuous improvement gains they were delivering, competitive metrics had ignited a new fire of motivation across the workforce, and increased role-clarity had de-clogged decision-making on important issues, creating a real sense of momentum in previously stalled areas. What's more, leaders now saw and knew how to use cultural levers as powerful drivers of business performance—catalyzed by the extraordinary results delivered by the business initiatives that were explicitly infused with cultural interventions.

CULTURE:
AT A GLANCE

 WHY IS IT IMPORTANT?

- Culture drives performance.
- It's hard to copy.
- Under-managed, it can be your undoing.

 WHAT ARE THE BIG IDEAS?

- Focus on more than employee engagement.
- Shift underlying mindsets that drive behaviors.
- Use four high-impact levers to get the job done.

 HOW DO I MAKE IT HAPPEN?

- Follow a five-step process to influence culture change.

  Most commonly neglected action in each step:

  Aspire: Measure the outcomes and practices that matter.

  Assess: Powerfully reframe current limiting mindsets.

  Architect: Engage/mobilize influence leaders early.

  Act: Make change personal for a critical mass of leaders.

  Advance: Infuse desired shifts into people processes.

9

Chapter

How do I lead organization-wide transformational change?

Transformational Change:
A TIMELESS TOPIC

LOOK THROUGHOUT HISTORY and you will undoubtedly find numerous quotes regarding the importance of change, whether it's ancient philosophers such as Heraclitus proclaiming, "The only thing constant is change," or more recent historical figures such as Napoléon Bonaparte declaring, "One must change...if one wishes to maintain one's superiority," or politicians like John F. Kennedy suggesting, "Change is the law of life. And those who look only to the past or present are certain to miss the future."[1]

Perhaps the most over-used quote about change, which has become something of a cliché, is, "It is not the strongest nor the most intelligent who will survive but those who can best manage change." While this is typically credited to Charles Darwin, he didn't actually say this—the source is Leon C. Megginson, a Professor of Management at Louisiana State University who, in 1963, wrote this as part of his analysis of Darwin's text. Rather than taking away from the weight of the quote, we feel the revelation of its true source only magnifies it. That it made its way from the pages of a regional social science quarterly publication, where it was originally published, into such ubiquity (including a prominent placement in the stone floor of the headquarters of the California Academy of Sciences where the initial attribution to Darwin has since been removed!) is witness to the deep resonance of its sentiment with the human experience.

In 1947, German-American psychologist Kurt Lewin developed one of the first models to structure the change process. Lewin's three-stage process consisted of "unfreezing" (dismantling defense mechanisms), "moving" (towards the intended change), and "freezing" (stabilizing the new levels of performance).[2] In the last seventy years. Lewin's work has been built on by innumerable change-management models, yet at the heart of all of them is an attempt to address Lewin's observation that, "A change towards a higher level of group [organizational] performance is frequently short-lived: after a 'shot in the arm,' group life soon returns to the previous level."

The notion of helping leaders drive rapid, significant and lasting change at the organizational level (not just that of an individual or a team) is fundamental to how we think about transformational change. A popular and apt analogy is that of a caterpillar turning into a butterfly. But why is this change a "transformation," whereas, say, the changing of state from water to ice doesn't make the cut? Two features are at play: First, the whole organism has been permanently altered from deep within—it can't go back! Second, it is altered in ways that give it significantly more freedom to act and capability to both survive and thrive in its environment. If you want your change efforts to result in more than the organizational equivalent of a bigger, fuzzier caterpillar, read on...

TYPES OF TRANSFORMATIONAL CHANGE CHALLENGES

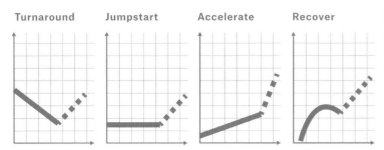

Turnaround   Jumpstart   Accelerate   Recover

Transformational change delivers a sustainable step-change improvement in organization-wide performance

Why is it important?
TRANSFORMATIONAL CHANGE
IS **A PATH TO GREATNESS**

MANY DISCUSSIONS on change begin with the dire statistics regarding how few transformation programs succeed. While it is indeed true (and we'll share those shortly!), we get far more excited about the upside of achieving transformational change. In this spirit, motivational speaker Joel Barker famously suggested, "Vision without action is merely a dream, action without vision merely passes the time, vision with action can change the world."[3] Transformational change is precisely that which connects vision to action—and enables companies to change the world for their customers, employees, shareholders, and the communities in which they operate.

In financial outcome terms, a recent study of company-wide transformation programs showed that, on average, the successful ones increase total return to shareholders (TRS) by 40 percent versus the market, earnings before interest and taxes (EBIT) by 4.3 times versus the starting point, returns on invested capital (ROIC) by 2.8 times, all delivered within thirty-six months of the launch of a transformation effort.[4]

Most people think of transformational change in terms of legendary turnaround stories: be it Steve Jobs' reinvention of Apple as it faced imminent collapse, Anne Mulcahy's bold "back to basics" approach to bringing Xerox back from the brink of bankruptcy, or Ravi Kant's tumultuous reversal of Tata Motors' fortunes. Like a Hollywood blockbuster, these were companies up against the ropes, and the punches were coming fast and furiously from stakeholders. Somehow, some way, however, herculean strength was conjured and bold risks taken and rewarded. And voilà, a world champion was (re)born! Of course each of these stories has unique complexities and sub-plots, but they are all about triumphantly restoring a company to its former glory.

Most leaders, however, face a different challenge. It's not about turning around the company, but taking it from what Jim Collins' calls "good to great." They have to find ways to create transformation when times are good. In these cases, the inertia to maintain the same level of thinking and behaving is strong. Sure, failure to act today could lead to a slow decline and eventual crisis situation. But on the flipside transformational change is hard—the day-to-day work of the business has to be carried out whilst the business is fundamentally rethought and changed. What's more, success is far from guaranteed (after all, "if it ain't broke, why fix it?"). At the far end of this spectrum is the type of challenge that Tim Cook of Apple and Jeff Immelt at GE are facing. How do you take a company at the top of its game to a whole new level—something we call a "great to greater still" transformation.

Regardless of the type of challenge, the goal is greatness, and the leaders who achieve this can be considered nothing short of great leaders.

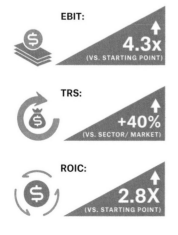

Average performance improvement achieved thirty-six months after the start of a successful program

Why is it important?
"CHANGE OR DIE" IS TRUE

CHANGE OR DIE, by Alan Deutschman, is one of the most attention-grabbing business book titles of all time. It is based on numerous studies that have found that most people don't change their lifestyles...even when their lives depend on it. Consider the predicament of people with heart disease. Years of research has shown that most cardiac patients can live considerably longer if they change their routines by cutting out smoking and drinking, eating less fat, reducing their stress levels, and exercising. Yet even though many make a real effort to do so, studies show 90 percent of people who have undergone surgery for heart disease revert to unhealthy behaviors within two years.

As with people, so it is with organizations. We've talked previously about the benefits of being in crisis to motivate change—but the fact is that even when survival is at stake, more often than not, organizations don't make the shift. Pan Am, Blockbuster, British Leyland, Lehman Brothers, WorldCom, Compaq, General Foods, Arthur Andersen, and Digital Equipment Corporation are all examples of once iconic companies that couldn't stop themselves from falling prey to bankruptcy or acquisition.

Which of today's household names will have ceased to exist in ten or twenty years' time? With massive changes in workforce demographics, acceleration in the scope, scale, and economic impact of technology, the complex interconnectivity of capital flows, and the increased volatility and unpredictability of capital markets, consumer confidence, and government policies, no company can take survival for granted. As management thinker Gary Hamel put it, "As the barriers that used to protect incumbents from the forces of creative destruction crumble and fall, once great companies increasingly find themselves on the defensive...over-dependent on customer ignorance, distribution monopolies, knowledge asymmetries, and other fast-disappearing sources of economic friction."[5]

Even if it doesn't mean the end of a company, market-leadership positions are increasingly precarious. Consider how long a typical company stays on the Standard & Poor's 500 stock market index: in 1958 the average was sixty-one years; by 1980, it was only twenty-five; fast forward to 2011 and the number of years had dropped to eighteen. A S&P 500 company in this decade is being replaced once every two weeks, which translates to roughly 75 percent of today's firms being superseded by newcomers in the index in the next ten years.[6]

Need more convincing? Have a look at the showcase companies that appeared in two of the most popular management books of the twentieth century, *In Search of Excellence* and *Built to Last*, and you'll find that only a third remain high performers, roughly 50 percent are struggling, and the rest no longer exist. Of course, all of these numbers are partly driven by macro-economic forces, industry attractiveness, and sheer luck. But for those companies that did survive and thrive, a good strategy and the ability to drive organization-wide transformational change to implement it are undoubtedly keys to success.

How long an average company stays in the S&P 500

PERCENTAGE OF 2017 **S&P 500** THAT ARE UNLIKELY TO BE IN THE **2027 INDEX**

Why is it important?
THERE IS A **PROVEN WAY** TO DOUBLE THE ODDS OF SUCCESS

THE ODDS of you winning the lottery aren't great, yet shockingly in the United States more money is spent on lottery tickets than on books, video games, recorded music, and tickets for movies and sporting events combined.[7] What if there was a proven way to more than double one's odds of winning the lottery—would people care? You bet they would! On a more somber note, the odds of dying in a motor vehicle accident over the span of your entire life is surprisingly high—1 in 113 in the United States.[8] What if there was a proven way to cut your chances of dying in half, would you want to know? We suspect so.

We've already established that there is both a huge upside and downside for organizations when it comes to whether or not they can make transformational change happen at scale. But what are the odds that you'll get it right? In the 1996 international bestseller *Leading Change*, John Kotter shared one of the most thoroughly researched answers at the time: only 30 percent of companies are able to lead effective transformational change programs. Since then, numerous academics and organizations have conducted similar research, and found similar results.[9] What's more, in spite of the fact that over 25,000 books on organizational change have been written since Kotter offered his advice on how to beat the odds and hundreds of business schools have built change management into their curricula, astoundingly the odds haven't improved in the last twenty years. It seems that, despite prolific output, the field of change management hasn't led to more successful change programs.

If there was a way for you as a leader to beat the odds, would you want to know about it? We hope so! The facts indicate there is indeed such an approach, and that using it improves your odds of success from 30 percent to 79 percent.[10] The methodology is the result of one of the most extensive research efforts ever undertaken in the field including: surveys of over three million employees in over 1,500 global organizations; reviews of over 900 books and top-tier articles on the topic of change; conducting over 100 cross-industry roundtable change leaders' forums; field-testing specific tools and techniques in over 100 companies; and closely following thirty CEOs as they led multi-year change journeys.

We're not saying transformational change is easy. To paraphrase C. S. Lewis, "It may be hard for a caterpillar to become a butterfly, but it's a jolly sight harder for it to learn to fly without wings."[11] We are saying, however, that there is a reliable method by which to create the wings on which your company can fly—the big ideas which we turn to now.

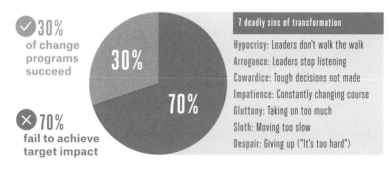

30% of change programs succeed

70% fail to achieve target impact

7 deadly sins of transformation

Hypocrisy: Leaders don't walk the walk
Arrogance: Leaders stop listening
Cowardice: Tough decisions not made
Impatience: Constantly changing course
Gluttony: Taking on too much
Sloth: Moving too slow
Despair: Giving up ("It's too hard")

Common pitfalls in leading transformational change

What are the big ideas?

PLACE EQUAL FOCUS ON
PERFORMANCE AND HEALTH

IN 1996 the Sunbeam Corporation, a U.S. manufacturer of electrical appliances, was in need of transformational change. Its earnings had been declining since December of 1994, and its stock was down 52 percent. Enter Al Dunlap, a proven turnaround artist who had taken over companies such as Scott Paper and Crown Zellerbach in similar situations, rapidly restructured them to make them profitable, and sold them off—much to the delight of shareholders. Such was his reputation that, on being named CEO and Chairman, the stock price rose 49 percent.

Dunlap quickly got to work—putting in place a new executive team (retaining only one original member), enacting massive layoffs to get costs down, and rationalizing the product portfolio. His swift action was rewarded by the stock price climbing 284 percent in his first seven months. Once the cost-cutting was done, Dunlap announced a growth strategy focused on five core product categories, increased customer segmentation, and differentiation on service. The stock soared to over three times where it started under his tenure.

After eighteen months in the role, Dunlap declared the turnaround complete and hired an investment bank to find a buyer. Only this time, unlike his previous turnarounds, there wasn't one. Ironically, the company's stock price had risen so high it sabotaged his plans to sell the company. Dunlap was now going to have to manage the company he turned around. In early 1998, Sunbeam began to post significant losses and in June, Dunlap became the next person cut.

Sunbeam's story is a cautionary tale in transformational change in that it illustrates what can happen when management focus on driving business performance is out of balance with improving organizational health. When driving change, most leaders naturally gravitate towards performance and its levers: how do I deliver shareholder and customer impact in financial and operational terms? In shorthand, we call these "buy, make, sell" questions—related to how to buy better/cheaper raw materials, make them into better/cheaper products or services, and sell them more effectively/efficiently into the market.

Equally important, however, is a focus on organizational health—ensuring an organization not only sustains step-change results but also continuously improves over time. We call questions related to health "align, execute, renew" questions: how do I align the organization on what needs to be done and why; execute with rigor and minimum interpersonal friction; and better equip the organization to renew itself over time, faster than the competition?

We use the terms performance and health, but others may prefer to use terms such as technical and adaptive, hard and soft, right and left brain, operational and cultural, or business and behavioral. Whatever the words you choose, the bottom line is that the success of your transformational change efforts will be far greater if you focus on both equally—longitudinal studies show this to be true to the tune of delivering 1.82 times the sustainable impact of approaches that emphasize one versus the other.[12]

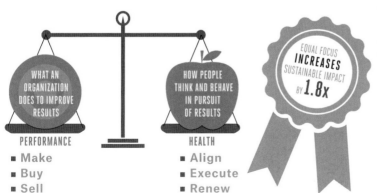

What we mean by performance and health

What are the big ideas?
APPLY THE **"FIVE FRAMES"** APPROACH

PUTTING EQUAL BALANCE on performance and health resonates with most leaders, yet 81 percent report that they don't know what this means they should actually do in practice. The answer is to use the "Five Frames" approach. This method takes our recommended five-step "5A's" approach to change that we've used throughout this book and provides one framework for performance, and one framework for health, in each of the steps. In total, then, there are five frameworks for performance, and five frameworks for health* that, if applied rigorously, unlock organization-wide transformational change:

STEP 1—ASPIRE: This stage answers, "Where do we want to go?" It starts by setting a strategic aspiration and specific performance objectives (performance frame 1). It then determines what health/behavior changes are required to enable impact to be achieved (health frame 1).

STEP 2—ASSESS: Before diving into creating the plan to achieve the aspiration, it's vital to first ask the question, "How ready are we to go there?" This identifies any institutional capability gaps that need to be filled (performance frame 2) and uncovers the critical few root-cause mindset shifts that will unlock desired behavior change (health frame 2).

STEP 3—ARCHITECT: This is all about "what we need to do to get there" in terms of the specific business initiatives to implement (performance frame 3) and how to reshape the work environment (through role-modeling, storytelling, skill- and confidence-building, and formal mechanisms) to influence mindsets (health frame 3).

STEP 4—ACT: Here the implementation journey is dynamically managed by piloting and scaling up initiatives (performance frame 4) as well as generating energy for the change via on-going communications, change leader actions, monitoring/review, empowerment, etc. (health frame 4).

STEP 5—ADVANCE: This step transitions work from being part of a transformation program into the day-to-day operation by embedding a continuous improvement infrastructure (performance frame 5) and ensuring leadership mastery has been built to take the company forward (health frame 5). While mentioned at the end of the transformational change process, the leadership capability is actually built by using steps 1–4 explicitly as a leadership development accelerator; it's in step 5 that that capacity is ready to be fully unleashed.

This may sound like a lot to manage—and it is! We make no apologies for this as we believe it abides by Einstein's edict that everything should be made as simple as possible, but no simpler.

TRANSFORMATION STEPS	PERFORMANCE FRAMES	HEALTH FRAMES
ASPIRE Where do we want to go?	Strategic Objectives	Health Targets
ASSESS How ready are we to go there?	Capability Platform	Underlying Mindsets
ARCHITECT What do we need to do to get there?	Portfolio of Initiatives	Influence Model
ACT How do we manage the journey?	Delivery Methods	Energy Generation
ADVANCE How do we keep moving forward?	Continuous Improvement	Centered Leadership

The Five Frames of transformational change

*Savvy readers will recognize that the health-side of transformational change overlaps significantly with what we covered in our chapter on culture. As such, more detail can be found there.

What are the big ideas?
BE RATIONAL ABOUT IRRATIONALITY

NOBEL-PRIZE-WINNING physicist and co-founder of the Santa Fe Institute, Murray Gell-Mann, once said, "Think how hard physics would be if particles could think."[13] His sentiment captures the importance, and complexity, of dealing with the human side of the change equation. This is precisely why systematically addressing health with equal rigor to performance is so important to success. Yet most leaders find their "textbook" efforts to address the human factors miss the mark: messages are sent but not heard, actions misunderstood, and incentives create unintended consequences.

The reason? The "particles" in the physics of transformational change (your employees) aren't just able to think...they very often do so irrationally. This is at the heart of why the change equation is hard to solve by even the smartest, most hard-working and well-intentioned leaders. There is a silver lining, however, in that we can predict human irrationality in many areas, thanks to research by social scientists. Knowing this, savvy leaders can use irrationality to accelerate vs. derail their change efforts.

Consider one of Daniel Kahneman's experiments involving a lottery run with a twist. Half of the participants were randomly assigned a lottery ticket. The remaining half were given a blank piece of paper and asked to write on it any number they pleased. Just before the winning number was drawn, researchers offered to buy back the tickets from their holders. The question they wanted to answer was how much more would have to be paid to those who "wrote their own number" than those who received one randomly. The rational answer would have been no difference at all, given a lottery is pure chance (every ticket, written or given, has the same odds). What did they actually find? Regardless of geography or demographics, they had to pay at least five times more to those who wrote their own number.

The lesson for leaders of transformational change? If you want to increase the motivation for (and therefore speed of) execution, it pays to involve others in creating the strategy, even when the answer may already be clear in the mind of the leader.

Further examples of predictable irrationality abound. We've also touched on a number of these in previous chapters, such as the importance of fair process over fair outcome (e.g. the "ultimatum game"), the motivational benefits of focusing on strengths versus deficits (e.g. the two bowling teams), and how people already think they are the change you're looking for (e.g. our treatment of the "self-serving bias").

The field of economics has already been transformed with the advent of behavioral economics, offering an improved understanding of how humans are predictably irrational. It's high time the same transformation happens within the practice of change management!

 You're best off letting others write their own story (5x more ownership is achieved when people create vs. being told)

 What motivates you doesn't necessarily motivate others (80% are driven by different sources of meaning than you are)

 Fair process matters (when it's missing, employees will often act against their own self interest, even if outcomes are fair)

 Money is the most expensive way to motivate (small, unexpected rewards invoke a stronger desire to reciprocate with action)

 Building on strengths gets you more than addressing weaknesses (2x more impact is achieved by leveraging what's working)

 Influencers aren't who you think they are (60% of leaders misjudge who the informal influencers are in their organization)

 Ask employees to improve, not to be the best (most believe they are already doing well, and it's others that have to change!)

Important lessons for transformational change from social science

How do I make it happen?
FOLLOW A **FIVE-STEP** **PROCESS** TO TRANSFORM

A LATIN-AMERICAN insurance company had fallen on challenging times. Its previously privileged position in the national market was unwinding due to regulation, mono-line attackers were taking advantage of new technologies to steal share in specific, high-margin product types, and customer buying patterns were moving towards direct channels where the company didn't have a strong presence. After a second year of losses, a new CEO was chosen by the owners with a mandate to drive organization-wide transformational change.

1. Aspire

THE FIRST STEP was to face facts. Over the course of eight weeks an intensive effort took stock of the company's competitive position, customer trends, shareholder expectations, cost benchmarks (internal and external), and the potential impacts of regulatory and technology trends. The company also looked at its health by benchmarking themselves using the OHI (Organizational Health Index) survey, conducting interviews and focus groups, and doing targeted analyses in areas such as pay for performance, turnover, and complexity.

This fact base culminated in a professionally facilitated "mirror workshop" where the senior team aligned on their current state and rolled up their sleeves together to set an aspiration for the future. The vision was coined "1 on 3 in 5": to be number one in the industry on profitability, client service, and employer of choice dimensions within a five-year timeframe. They also identified the three management practices—prioritization, empowerment, and accountability—that would increase their organizational health to enable the change to happen as efficiently, effectively, and sustainably as possible.

Aspire
Where do we want to go?

 **Strategic objectives**
- Understand context and baseline
- Identify opportunity areas
- Set overall aspiration

 Health targets
- Create a shared language and baseline
- Establish relevant health targets
- Align the top team

2. Assess

DURING THE NEXT eight weeks, the capabilities that were strategically important to deliver on the overall aspiration were identified and the current state of each was then diagnosed against technical, management, and behavioral systems required for them to be distinctive. In order to ensure there was no over-estimation, a third-party view was included in the assessment. Finally, options for building the capabilities were pulled together. In parallel, specialized interview techniques and qualitative data analysis were employed to uncover the underlying mindsets that explained why employees were choosing to perpetuate dysfunctional management practices.

All of the findings and recommendations were then worked through in depth by the top team during a second workshop, which lasted a day and a half. Coming out of the session there was full alignment and deep conviction to prioritize capability-building efforts in four areas: managing agent productivity, risk-adjusted pricing and underwriting, sub-segment direct channel product offerings, and lean cost management. What's more, three mindsets were determined to be the root cause of why smart, hard-working employees somehow all agreed on the dysfunctions in the organization, yet were complicit in letting them play out day in and day out. These included a belief that "failure is not an option" (vs. "success is the far side of being willing to fail small and fast"), "criticism damages relationships" (vs. "honesty builds trust"), and "work hard and tend to the details" (vs. "have impact and focus on what matters").

Assess
How ready are we to go there?

◎ Capability platform
 • Define capability requirements
 • Take stock of current state
 • Prioritize what, when, how

 Underlying mindsets
 • Prioritize behavior change required
 • Identify root-cause mindsets
 • Reframe strengths to address weaknesses

3. Architect

AT THIS POINT the top team wanted to engage a broader leadership coalition to "write their own lottery ticket" within the direction outlined. During a highly energetic two-day workshop with the top fifty leaders in the company, the results from the Aspire and Assess stages were internalized and refined. Then the large group went through an exercise of prioritizing potential performance initiatives to pursue over the next three years (fifteen in total), as well as brainstorming and selecting high-impact actions to shift mindsets and behaviors through role-modeling, story-telling, building skills and confidence, and formal mechanisms (changes to structure, processes, systems, and incentives).

Coming out of the workshop, small groups of leaders fleshed out the potential initiatives, being clear on the scope, potential impact, accountabilities, measurement mechanisms, rough budget and resource requirements, interdependencies, and major milestones. Examples of these initiatives included redesigning the claims management process, creating a mobile channel, selling non-core businesses, reducing overhead costs, upgrading underwriting and key account management capabilities, creating a new product suite in the auto segment, and so on. What's more, the teams working on each initiative were also accountable for "engineering" it "for health" by specifying how, in its content and/or in the process suggested to implement it, it would itself influence desired shifts in mindsets and behaviors as well as act as a leadership development accelerator for those involved.

At the same time, additional health-related actions were taken in the form of creating a compelling change story and an on-going communications campaign, modernizing the leadership standard to reflect performance and health aspirations, and changing performance contracts, incentives, and the management process that connected them together. Finally, a set of change leaders were identified (leveraging an elegantly simple e-mail chain approach to identify influence leaders) and plan for their mobilization developed.

Architect
What do we need to do to get there?

 **Portfolio of initiatives**
- Scope improvement initiatives
- Balance portfolio for risk, difficulty, and impact
- Sequence taking into account interdependencies

 Influence model
- Write change story
- Engage a broad leadership coalition
- Plan changes in formal mechanisms

4. Act

AFTER A FINAL workshop with the top team and top fifty leaders where the design was finalized, the program was launched with the top 500 leaders coming together for two days. The workshop was designed to enable them to go through a mini-version of the process that had taken place up to that point—looking at the performance and health mirror, understanding and internalizing the journey and decisions made linking the aspirations to the portfolio of initiatives and related culture-change game plan. The session was modeled around the chapters of the change story—who we are, why we need to change (and why now), where are we headed, how will we get there, what does it mean for me, and why does it matter?

After the session, the transformation plan was cascaded throughout the company's 40,000 collaborators over the next month. There were no elaborate PowerPoint presentations. Instead, before each session a pre-read assignment was sent with the full change story in prose such that when units got together they had a conversation about what they had read—leaders answered questions, the participants discussed what the implications were for their area/how they could make the biggest difference, and then reflected on and made individual commitments to one another related to how they would lead from the front.

The portfolio of initiatives was executed in three "300-day" waves. The first included initiatives aimed at restoring profitability, the second was about gaining growth momentum, and the third focused on accelerating to number one. Multiple deployment methods were used based on the nature of the initiative, most often the use of pilots and training forward leaders to then scale up efforts geometrically. While line ownership was a central feature, a five-person PMO team effectively ensured efforts stayed coordinated and could be monitored and reviewed at an overall program level. Change leaders and a very effective communications program, aimed at celebrating successes and sharing learnings through every channel possible (including monthly virtual interactive "CEO chats" with all leaders), effectively created and sustained energy.

Act
How do we manage the journey?

 Delivery methods
- Test, learn, and scale up initiatives
- Put in place line-led governance
- Establish PMO to support and enable

 **Energy Generation**
- Cascade and reinforce the change story
- Mobilize change leaders
- Engineer performance initiatives for health

5. Advance

AS THE COMPANY moved into the last of its 300-day waves, they had already achieved many of their objectives, and began to shift their efforts from driving the transformation to evolving their methods into a permanent working model that would deliver year-on-year continuous improvement. Processes were established to enable grass-roots business-improvement initiatives to be quickly surfaced, funded, and executed. The change leader group was refreshed with continuous improvement champions representing each major area. The PMO was wound down and the relevant target-setting and monitoring approaches built directly into the on-going strategic and annual budgeting processes, and centers of excellence were created to ensure knowledge would be captured and shared.

Perhaps most importantly, throughout the life of the program every leader down to the front-line had participated in a field and forum leadership development program that was integrated into the work of the initiatives. Also, although leaders were equipped with additional technical skills, the experiential coursework mostly focused on making personal mindset and behavior shifts, finding and creating meaning, turning challenges into opportunities through reframing, building a network of relationships, being proactive in the face of uncertainty, and managing energy as well as time (all aspects of the "Centered Leader" model). These attributes now permeated the culture and were built into the learning and development and role-modeling fabric of the organization.

Advance
How do we keep moving forward?

 Continuous improvement
- Set CI expectations
- Ensure best-practice sharing
- Implement organizational learning processes

 Centered leadership
- Use the transformation to develop leaders
- Employ "field and forum" techniques
- Identify and upskill next gen leaders

THREE YEARS AFTER the program began, to the delight of the leadership team and owners, the company had not only restored profitability and driven growth successfully, but had already achieved the number one market positions in all of the areas it had targeted. ROI was in double digits, margins were healthy, and market share was strong. What's more, the future looked bright as the health of the company was not just in the top quartile, but in the top 3 percent of all companies in the Organizational Health Index (OHI) database. The most profound shifts had been achieved in areas related to individual goals being aligned to company goals, behavior being driven by strategy, and overall motivation of the workforce.

TRANSFORMATIONAL CHANGE:
AT A GLANCE

WHY IS IT IMPORTANT?

- Transformational change is a path to greatness.
- "Change or die" is true.
- There is a proven way to double the odds of success.

WHAT ARE THE BIG IDEAS?

- Place equal focus on performance and health.
- Apply the "five-frames" approach.
- Be rational about irrationality.

HOW DO I MAKE IT HAPPEN?

- Follow a five-step process to transform.

  Most commonly neglected action in each step:

  Aspire: Engage a broad leadership coalition from day one.

  Assess: Focus equally on strengths and weaknesses.

  Architect: Engineer performance initiatives for health.

  Act: Tap into five sources of meaning for employees.

  Advance: Identify and upskill next-generation leaders.

Chapter **10**

How do I successfully transition into a new leadership role?

Leadership Transitions:
A TIMELESS TOPIC

BLACK TUESDAY, 1929. The U.S. stock market experiences the most devastating crash in history, signaling the beginning of the ten-year Great Depression that affected all Western industrialized countries. Between 1929 and 1932 the U.S. stock market plunged 85 percent, worldwide GDP fell by an estimated 15 percent (by comparison, during the recent "Great Recession" of 2008–2009 it fell 1 percent), international trade plunged more than 50 percent, and unemployment in some countries rose as high as 33 percent.

This was the context in which Franklin D. Roosevelt transitioned into the role of Chief Executive of the United States. He began his remarkable "first 100 days" by giving one of the most famous inaugural speeches in history declaring, "We have nothing to fear but fear itself." Four hours later, his cabinet was sworn in. Within twenty-four hours, he shut down the banking system and drafted an Emergency Banking Act. Within a week, the banking system was back in operation with the financial panic arrested. Over the course of the next three months, fifteen pieces of legislation were passed that reshaped America with a "new deal" of farm credits, federal works projects, and new financial regulations. All the while he spoke directly to the nation during his regular radio broadcast "fireside chats."

The speed and certainty with which Roosevelt conducted his transition echoes that of Julius Caesar in ancient times. Although Caesar is best known for his military conquests, in the words of Martin Armstrong, former Chairman of Princeton Economics International, "... after defeating all contenders, Caesar returned to Rome in 46 BC and began such a sweeping economic reform, that it puts to shame any accomplishments of the first 100 days that began with Roosevelt."[1] Caesar's actions ranged from reforming the labor market and justice system to furthering education and healthcare, dealing with the trade deficit, and creating a new calendar. Veni, vidi, vici ("I came, I saw, I conquered") indeed!

These are but two famous transitions among a myriad that have happened throughout history and will continue to happen as long as organizations exist. Every transition brings with it uncertainty. Will the new leader uncover and seize opportunities that their predecessors failed to? Will they spend their time in the right places? Will they put in place the right team? Will the changes they make be sustainable? Will they develop a worthy successor? And so on. Ultimately, the questions boil down to one: will they or won't they be successful?

Today, there are an estimated 8,000 senior executive transitions in the combined levels of CEO, CEO reports, and their reports in Fortune 500 companies alone. If you take our definition of a transition period as being the time it takes for a leader and their organization to be working at full productivity towards a shared outcome, the business value of getting transitions right is obvious. The faster a leader gets to full productivity, and the higher the magnitude of that productivity, the more value is created. If you want to get your transition right, or ensure your organization best supports leaders taking on new roles to get it right, read on...

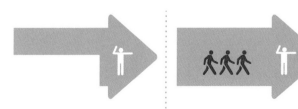

A leader is in transition until they and their organization are working at full productivity towards a shared outcome

Why is it important?

LEADERSHIP TRANSITIONS ARE **HIGH STAKES** EVENTS

YOU ARE TRANSITIONING into a new senior executive role, how do you feel? Of course context matters greatly in answering that question. Are you assuming a newly created position? Are you taking over from a particularly weak or a particularly strong leader? Are you coming in from the outside of the organization or area? Is this a big promotion or a lateral move? Is it in a business or functional area you know well? Is there a notice period so that you can prepare before you take the role, or is it a sudden move? Do you have an existing relationship with your boss and the team, and if so what is the nature of that relationship? And so on.

Regardless of context, an executive transition is typically a high-stakes event both in emotional and business terms. Emotionally, for the leader, there is a mix of excitement (e.g. the possibility to make a difference on a new/bigger stage, the chance to coach and develop a new generation of talent, increased self-esteem, and greater rewards from having been chosen) and apprehension (e.g. from high expectations, a more intense spotlight, increased complexity, and self-doubt in the face of a steep learning curve). In fact, when asked to rank life's challenges in order of difficulty, the top-ranked challenge is "making a transition at work" (ahead of other life events such as dealing with bereavement, a divorce, or health issues).[2] For those who placed the leader, there is the hope that they made the right choice, and the fear they've gotten it wrong. For those in the leader's organization, a transition opens up the destabilizing uncertainty of "What will this mean for me?"

On the business front, if the transition is successful, there is a high probability the leader's business will be successful in the long run. For example, nine out of ten teams whose leader was judged to have had a successful transition go on to meet their three-year performance goals. Moreover, the attrition risk for their teams is 13 percent lower, their teams show discretionary effort levels that are 2 percent higher, and they generate 5 percent more revenue and profit than average. On the flipside, the performance of direct reports to a leader who struggled in their transition is 15 percent lower than those who report to a high-performing one. What's more, these leaders are 20 percent more likely to be disengaged or leave the organization.[3]

In addition to productivity losses, there are also very direct transition costs. These costs vary widely depending on the context, but typically include any advertising and search costs, relocation, sign-on bonuses, referral awards, and the overhead of HR professionals and other leaders involved in the process, in addition to the aforementioned loss of productivity. Taken together, for senior executive roles these costs are estimated to be up to 213 percent of the position's annual salary.[4] Perhaps the most significant penalty is losing six, twelve, or eighteen months of moving the organization forward while the competition races ahead.

Big upside. Big downside. No matter how you look at it—whether you're the senior leader transitioning or the company managing the transition, it pays to get it right.

Successful transitions result in

90% higher likelihood of teams meeting three-year performance goals

13% less attrition risk

Unsuccessful transitions result in

20% less engagement

15% lower performance

The impact of successful and unsuccessful executive transitions

Search costs for a new executive are 213% of their annual salary

Why is it important?

NEARLY **HALF OF TRANSITIONS FAIL,** MOSTLY DUE TO THE SOFT STUFF

AT THE END of 2010, Ron Johnson was a star executive at Apple. As vice-president of retail operations, he pioneered the concept of the Apple Retail Stores and the Genius Bar. Previous to his ten years at Apple, he had made a name for himself as the vice-president of merchandizing for Target, where he was credited with making the store "hip."[5] Armed with an undergraduate degree from Stanford and an MBA from Harvard, he was a proven executive talent who had successfully navigated many transitions in his career. In November 2011, he was hired with great fanfare by the U.S. department store chain J. C. Penney, succeeding Mike Ullman who had served as CEO for the previous seven years.

Johnson radically overhauled the chain by putting an end to discounting and refashioning its stores as collections of boutiques for hip brands. His plan failed miserably. Sixteen months later, when he was relieved of his duties in early 2013, sales were down $6 billion, the stock price had declined 51 percent, the company had shed 40,000 employees, and was carrying enormous debt. In April 2013, Mike Ullman was brought back as CEO to reverse the damage done.

While most transitions don't fail as epically as Johnson's, studies show that, when viewed two years after the fact, between 27 and 46 percent of senior transitions are considered to be failures or underperforming versus expectations.[6] Keep in mind that these are senior leaders, who have demonstrated success and shown intelligence, initiative, and results in their previous roles. So why does this happen? The research is clear: 68 percent of transitions trip up on issues related to culture, people, and politics, 67 percent of leaders wish they had moved faster on changing the culture, and navigating organizational politics is ranked as the number one transition challenge by leaders. This isn't just a function of coming in from the outside either: 79 percent of external and 69 percent of internal hires report implementing culture change is difficult.[7,8,9]

But in Johnson's case, wasn't it a failure of strategy? After all, he angered frugal long-time customers by getting rid of discounting and didn't win new customers; meanwhile he spent hand over fist reconfiguring stores. Former HR head, Dan Walker, sees it differently, "I think the strategy was right on the money. We'll never know what the results would have been if we'd gotten to the point where the stores had largely been transformed."[10] Johnson himself observes that many remnants of his boutiques-in-store strategy are contributing to success today. As Fortune reports, "Johnson largely blames the company's stagnant culture for the failure, saying people were entrenched and resisting him."[11] Former COO Mike Kramer concurs that, culturally speaking, "It was like oil and water from day one." Johnson didn't help matters in the way he chose to handle the soft stuff. As Fortune reported about his leadership style, "Criticism, valid or otherwise, marked you as a skeptic."[12]

Leaders in transition are wise to heed leadership coach Marshall Goldsmith's advice that "What got you here won't get you there,"[13] in particular as it relates to the soft stuff.

27–46% of transitions fail (depending on which study you look at)

68% of transition failures are due to cultural issues

67% of leaders wish they moved faster on changing culture

65% of leaders rate navigating politics as the hardest part

How the soft stuff affects transition success rates

Why is it important?
TRANSITION FREQUENCY IS RISING, YET **LITTLE HELP IS ON OFFER**

GIVEN THE continually increasing pace and magnitude of change in the business world, it's not surprising to find that the rate of senior executive transitions is on the rise. Starting from the top, CEO turnover rates have increased from 11.6 percent in 2010 to 16.6 percent in 2015.[14] Sixty-nine percent of these new CEOs reshuffle their management teams within their first two years, causing a cascading number of transitions in senior ranks.[15] Recent studies show that 67 percent of leaders report that their organizations are experiencing "some or many more" transitions now than in the past year.[16]

So many transitions, so much value at stake. Surely every company would prioritize supporting these transitions to ensure they are a success? The facts suggest otherwise. Only 29 percent of leaders in the U.S., and 32 percent of leaders globally feel that their organizations support new leaders appropriately during transitions, and 74 percent of U.S. leaders and 83 percent of global leaders feel they arrive at their new roles underprepared.[17] As the CEB puts it, "Most organizations approach new leadership transitions in the same way many organizations approach mergers and acquisitions: as one-off events...The typical unsystematic "hands-off" transition approach relies heavily on new leaders to self-manage their transitions. However, most leaders experience only a handful of transitions during their careers, so for them, each transition remains more art than science."[18]

So what are organizations doing to support successful transitions? Research shows that the most common method is providing mentoring or informal "buddy" networks. Yet only 47 percent of external hires find these helpful; an even fewer 29 percent of internal hires find these helpful. The second most common support method is through standard orientation programs, which only 19 percent of external and 11 percent of internal executives report as effective. There are methods that are proven to double the likelihood of a successful transition, such as customized assimilation plans and programs and tailored executive coaching, but these are only provided by 32 percent of organizations.[19,20] When asked what additional support organizations plan on providing in the future, the number one response is to expand the expectations of the HR business partner to play a support role. The catch, of course, is that HR business partners report they already have full plates without devoting more attention to transition needs.[21]

If you were an operations manager increasing production rates and 29 to 47 percent of the products coming off your production line had defects, you'd swarm on fixing the problem. The same logic has to apply to senior executive transitions, in particular given the potential upside benefits. Read on to find out "what" and "how" to do so...

More transitions

43% higher CEO turnover rates today than 5 years ago

67% of leaders are experiencing "some or many more" transitions than in the past

Too little support

Less than **1/3** of leaders feel that their organizations support leaders in transition appropriately

Roughly **3/4** of leaders report that they are under-prepared for their roles

Indicators of executive transition frequency and support

What are the big ideas?

TAKE STOCK AND TAKE ACTION IN FIVE AREAS SIMULTANEOUSLY

MIGUEL DE CERVANTES, widely regarded as the greatest writer in the Spanish language, once wrote, "To be prepared is half the battle." When it comes to your transition into a senior leadership role, we agree. So what's the other half? Another famous Spaniard, artist Pablo Picasso, puts it well in saying, "Action is the foundational key to success." Indeed, leaders are well advised to think of their transitions in two equal steps: First, take stock; then, take action. In our experience these two steps should happen across each of the following five dimensions:

YOUR BUSINESS/FUNCTION: Do you have a clear read on the current state of performance and capability (take stock), and have you aligned and mobilized your team and the organization on the aspiration and priorities going forward (take action)?

CULTURE: Do you understand the current state of the culture and any shifts required to unlock future performance (take stock), and are you influencing those shifts with all of the levers available to you and your team (take action)?

TEAM: Do you have the right team configuration in terms of the skill and will present in your team members and the right structure to work in (take stock), and have you embarked on a structured journey to become a high-performing team (take action)?

YOURSELF: Have you done what it takes personally to get up to speed, set boundaries, and consider the legacy you want to leave in the role (take stock), and are you spending your time wisely playing the role that only you can play (take action)?

OTHER STAKEHOLDERS: Do you understand your mandate and the other expectations major stakeholders have of you (take stock), and have you established a productive working rhythm and relationship with them to continue to shape their views (take action)?

Beware of generic answers to these questions. Every leader's starting point will be different. For some their role will be largely to maintain and steadily improve what they've inherited in each of the dimensions, for others transformational change will be required on all fronts, and for others it will be a mix. Take, for example, what has become almost axiomatic advice that CEOs should replace 50 percent of the team to make it "their team." In fact, 72 percent of CEOs taking over poorly-performing companies and 66 percent of those taking over high-performing companies do exactly that. The benefits of doing so, however, vary greatly. The poorly-performing companies enjoy an increase of +0.8 percent Total Return to Shareholders, while the high-performing companies destroy value.[22] Every leader needs to put the right team together, but how best to do so will be unique to each situation.

Managing the five focus areas simultaneously isn't easy. Like spinning plates, do it too slowly and the plates lose momentum and crash to the ground, too fast and they spin out of control. Get it right, and a spectacular success is achieved.

	TAKE STOCK	TAKE ACTION
1. BUSINESS	Current state, trends, and opportunities	Alignment on aspirations and priorities
2. CULTURE	Current state, desired shifts	Using four levers to influence
3. TEAM	Right people and configuration	Becoming high-performing
4. MYSELF	My expectations, getting up to speed	Playing the role only I can
5. STAKEHOLDERS	Understanding and shaping mandate	Productive rhythm and relationship

Topics to tackle in taking stock and taking action

What are the big ideas?
BE AS CLEAR ON **WHAT YOU WON'T DO** AS WHAT YOU WILL

WHEN ALAN G. LAFLEY took the helm at Proctor & Gamble in June 2000, the global consumer goods giant was floundering. His predecessor had issued three profit warnings in four months and P&G had become the worst performing company in the Dow Industrial Index. Much has been written about what Lafley did to increase profits by 70 percent and revenues by almost 30 percent in the first five years of his tenure, but the success is as much about what he stopped as what he started. He and his senior management team stringently prioritized four core businesses and ten out of more than 100 countries. He put a swift end to almost US$200 million of "skunk works" experimental technology projects and ended regional marketing campaigns. And so on.

Lafley sums up his philosophy in saying, "Make the direction Sesame Street simple so it can be understood broadly...also be clear on what you won't do—what needs to stop...Most human beings and most companies don't like to make choices, and they particularly don't like to make a few choices they really have to live with...If we caught people doing stuff we said we were not going to do, we would pull the budget and the people and we'd get them refocused on what we said we were going to do." [23] His philosophy is strikingly similar to that of former Apple CEO, Steve Jobs, who said, "I'm as proud of what we don't do as I am of what we do."[24] Along the same lines, management thinker Jim Collins notes that great companies create a "stop doing" list to complement their "to do" list.[25]

In our experience, one of the most common traps that senior executives in new roles fall into is not being as clear on what the direction under their leadership isn't as what it is. Why? Because here's what happens otherwise: employees hear what the new direction is and first reframe what they are already doing to show how it fits into the new direction; next they see opportunities to put forward pet projects as a way to advance the aspiration...and in doing so overload the organization with well-intentioned but fragmented efforts. As the initiative lists swell, impact slows, leadership commitment fades, and momentum is lost. The facts back up the philosophy. Successful leaders are 1.8 times more likely than others to have explicitly communicated what their expectations were about what to stop, as well as what to start.[26]

As leaders in transition "take stock," they are wise to ask about what others would like to see change or not change, but also to explicitly question what should slow down, be delayed, or stop—whether initiatives, meetings, process steps, reports, or rituals. As they "take action," they should not only be clear about will stop and start, but also adopt an on-going philosophy from the world of good housekeeping: One in, one out. If one new shirt goes into your closet, which old shirt should be discarded to make room? Similarly, when a new initiative is proposed, the question isn't simply "what's the business case?", but also "what will we stop doing to create the time, money, resource, and focus on doing this well?"

% of respondents	ORGANIZATION UNDERSTANDS NEW LEADER'S PRIORITIES	ORGANIZATION UNDERSTANDS WHAT NEW LEADER PLANS TO STOP	
Successful transitions	60%	60%	*The impact of having a "stop doing" list*
Unsuccessful transitions	32%	34%	

"I'm as proud of what we don't do as I am of what we do."
– Steve Jobs, former CEO, Apple

What are the big ideas?

FORGET "100 DAYS"—BE IMPACT-DRIVEN, NOT CALENDAR-DRIVEN

YOU'VE JUST moved from Rome to Mexico City. To celebrate, you're cooking dinner for a group of new friends. Unfortunately, things didn't go as planned—the pasta was undercooked, the bread dry, and the dessert too hard on the outside, too soft in the center. You neglected to take into account that you're cooking at an altitude 2,200 meters higher than usual. This means lower air pressure, causing foods to take longer to bake, water to boil at a lower temperature, and gases to expand more. The next day you go for your morning run. You normally power through six kilometers in 30 minutes, but today you can barely make five. What gives (it's not that you overate the night before!)? Turns out the reduced oxygen levels at high altitude are getting the best of you.

The point? How long something should take depends on context. And with all of the contextual variables involved, the time it should take for a leader to get to full productivity will be unique to their transition. Yet if you type "executive transitions" into Amazon, you'll find a daunting list of books offering 90-day and 100-day plans for success. They all offer much the same message: you have a limited period to get to full productivity as a leader, and if you don't make it in time, you're doomed. Such an approach may make for good marketing, but it isn't supported by the evidence. In practice, most new leaders—92 percent of external hires and 72 percent of internal hires—take far more than ninety days to get up to full productivity.[27] What's more, many executives admit that it took them at least six months to achieve real impact (62 percent for external, 25 percent for internal hires).

Taking an outside-in look at expectations confirms the first 100 days as an artificial construct. For example, for new CEOs, stakeholders typically look for a new strategic vision to be shared in the first eight months and give them fourteen months to get their new team in place. The time to see an increase in share price has an even longer expectation runway of nineteen months.[28] This doesn't mean leaders should wait to act. For example, 72 percent of leaders wish they had moved faster on their teams. On the other hand, leaders should not feel pressured to act too soon. More than half of executives reflect that they didn't spend enough time taking stock of the personal leadership strengths and weaknesses and thinking through their target personal operating model as part of their transitions.[29]

The very concept of the "first 100 days" in transition is often tied back to the U.S. president Franklin D. Roosevelt, whose story we shared at the start of this chapter. The irony is that when he coined the phrase he wasn't referring to his transition, but to the 100 days he kept Congress in session without adjournment to pass the bulk of the New Deal legislation. General Electric CEO, Jeff Immelt, sums up the ultimate takeaway for leaders, "All these books about the first 90 [or 100] days are kind of rubbish in many ways."[30] Read on to understand how an impact-driven vs. calendar-driven approach is far more likely to make your transition a success...

Time it takes to become fully productive, % of leaders reporting

More than 90 days — 100%
72%

More than 6 months — 62%
25%

■ External hire
■ Internal hire

Number of months given to a CEO to...

Develop a strategic vision 8
Win support of employees 9
Build the right team 14
Earn credibility with analysts 17
Increase share price 19
Turn company around 21
Reinvent how the company does business 22

How long it really takes to successfully transition

How do I make it happen?

FOLLOW A **FIVE-STEP PROCESS** TO SUCCESSFULLY TRANSITION

SOFIA, A SENIOR LEADER at a European financial services company, just accepted a Senior Executive position in their insurance brokerage business. Her career trajectory had been closely observed by the leadership, and they felt that although it would be a stretch assignment for her, she was the right one for the role. Sofia started in the finance department of the retail banking unit and moved quickly through the ranks by taking on a series of increasingly challenging corporate roles. She had had some contact with the insurance business, but knew little of how its operation worked. She was well aware, however, of the business's reputation as a weak performer.

1. Aspire

AS SOON AS SOFIA accepted the new role, she immersed herself in the details. She spent time understanding the outgoing leader's views, listening carefully while bearing in mind that performance was below par during his tenure. She also organized a session with third-party experts to get primed on industry dynamics, competitor trends, and best practices. In addition, she met up with a couple of colleagues from earlier in her career who now worked in the same business, and she started to get to know the team she was inheriting.

Once in the role, Sofia began to engage the organization, spending time in the field visiting the regional offices.

While there, she interviewed high-performing employees individually to get their advice and met with the rest of the staff. She also met key customer accounts to hear their hopes and concerns. Meanwhile, on her behalf, a small group was pulling together a baseline analysis of the business unit's performance and culture. She met the team every week to discuss findings and create "one version of the truth."

Ten weeks into the role, Sofia brought her team together for a two-day "aspiration-setting" offsite. In advance, members received the baseline information about the business so that they could use their time productively to focus on the work that only they could do. Together they co-created a high-level aspiration: "We will operate as a bank-owned business, not a standalone company," "We will be disciplined in our segmentation rather than being everything to everyone," and "We will show that we can grow organically and only then consider further acquisitions." They also agreed to an interim modus operandi of biweekly meetings to deepen their discussion.

Aspire
Where do we want to go?

- **Baseline:** Create a "one version of the truth" that holds up the mirror to:
  - Competitive dynamics
  - Historic performance
  - Current culture
  - Industry dynamics
- **Listening tour:** Spend time in the field with stakeholders
- **Co-create:** Engage your team in co-creating a high-level aspiration and path to flesh it out

2. Assess

WITH THE CURRENT state and high-level aspiration clear and aligned on, Sofia and her strategy team identified the priority areas that should be focused on to achieve their aspiration. The team also identified that new capabilities were needed—digital marketing, data analytics, CRM. Finally, various options for the best organization design to deliver against the new priorities were considered. Twelve weeks into her new job, Sofia announced a restructuring of the business, the early retirement of two executives, and the creation of three new roles on her executive team.

During this time, Sofia spent an hour every morning catching up informally with key stakeholders. Meanwhile, she also had a small team running several focus groups to identify potential limiting mindsets and behaviors that could interfere with their aspiration. They found that many employees felt that being part of a larger financial services institution inhibited the insurance operation's performance rather than giving it a competitive advantage. Employees also lacked trust in the capabilities of colleagues outside their own department. There was also a widespread belief that "everything else (including margin) takes care of itself as long as revenue is growing."

In the next workshop with her team, an experienced facilitator helped them reach agreement on specific performance goals, such as margin growth, cross-sell rates, and customer satisfaction, and identify the necessary mindset and behavior shifts.

Assess
How ready are we to go there?

- **Targets:** Specify value drivers to deliver the aspiration.
- **Capabilities:** Understand the gap between current and required.
- **Mindsets:** Determine what "from/to" shifts are needed in mindsets and behaviors.
- **Early wins:** Make "no regrets" changes to structures and people.
- **Stakeholder engagement:** Spend more time in the field with stakeholders.
- **Team alignment:** Engage your team in co-creating "from/to" objectives for priority areas.

3. Architect

HAVING "TAKEN STOCK" of the situation and aligned on an aspiration, Sofia and her new team began to plan how they would "take action" to move the organization forward. Initiative teams were launched to scope out what would happen in each priority area. Executive-level members acted as sponsors for each initiative, working in pairs so as to get to know each other better. The initiative teams were focused on defining a customer-segmentation strategy, optimizing technology resources, standardizing office models and compensation structures, and creating more integrated partnerships with other businesses in the company. Not only were they expected to come back with traditional business cases, but also to propose "what should stop," how the needed capabilities were being built, and how the initiative was explicitly "engineered for culture change" through actions related to role-modeling, storytelling, reinforcing mechanisms, and skill-building.

At the next offsite, the scope of each initiative was discussed and signed off. The work was also reviewed from a programmatic perspective—what were the key decisions that would need to be made, what were the overall milestones, and what governance mechanisms would be used? A few scenarios were worked through to ensure everyone understood decision rights, key performance indicators, and interdependencies going forward. Then the full picture of why, what, how, when, and who of the entire program of work was put together in the form of a change story. Finally, the team discussed what their role needed to be and decided on their steady-state operating rhythm going forward.

Architect
What do we need to do to get there?

- **Initiatives:** Launch strategic initiative teams with senior sponsors
- **Change management:** Determine plan for culture change and change management
- **Stop doing:** Specify what will change and what won't (or shouldn't)
- **Change story:** Combine elements into an integrated change story
- **Commitments:** Discuss individual and team leadership commitments
- **Cadence:** Determine an operating rhythm for running the business

4. Act

AFTER THE OFFSITE, Sofia rapidly turned her sights to making detailed plans in parallel with getting some quick wins on the board. She created a program management office (PMO) role to coordinate the various initiative teams to get the work done. This phase would culminate in an offsite with the top 300 leaders in the organization, at which point the overall change story and detailed implementation plans would be shared and refined. In order that the session would formally mark the launch of the new direction for the organization, the PMO was tasked with fleshing out a full change-management and communications plan. In the meantime, the Finance and HR teams reviewed current business and talent processes to ensure their alignment with the new direction and to clarify "who was on the hook for what."

For her part, Sofia spent time with her boss, Rajit, ensuring he was comfortable and supportive of the plan. She also asked that he play a role in kicking off the offsite with the top 300, putting the potential of the new direction in the context of what it would mean for the company overall. She also worked with her assistant to put guidelines on her calendar, ensuring that she would be devoting time to the important as well as ensuring enough flex was built in to deal with the urgent.

Act
How do we manage the journey?

- **Leadership alignment:** Align a broader senior leadership coalition (e.g. top 300) on aspiration and priorities
- **Influence leaders:** Find and mobilize change leaders down through the line to make progress
- **Measurement:** Implement required measurement and review capabilities
- **Process:** Build new direction into business- and talent-management processes, ensuring personal accountabilities are clear
- **Role modeling:** Personally role model desired change

5. Advance

WITH THE TOP 300 leaders' session behind her, Sofia began to move from a transition mode into more of a steady-state approach to driving the business forward. In the next six months, she continued her monthly meetings with the PMO, steering committee, and initiative teams, and then switched to a quarterly schedule once things were well on track. She continued to stay on top of her personal time management, ensuring she proactively balanced how much she spent with customers, business partners, regulators, and team coaching, while holding back enough time to reflect on strategy, the organization's dynamics, and her personal impact.

Sofia stayed close to her team both as a whole and through frequent one-on-one coaching sessions to ensure they remained fully on board. She was disappointed that six months into her role there were two leaders who had not changed as she'd hoped, and she proceed to make the needed changes. This was made easier by the fact that she had worked with her head of Human Resources to ensure there were succession options, in particular in vulnerable areas. She also drew on an inner circle of informal advisors who she used as a sounding board, a source of discreet advice, and an avenue to get "the real scoop" on how her and her team's actions were being perceived deeper into the organization.

Advance
How do we keep moving forward?

- **Personal renewal**: Ensure you focus personal time on priorities and renewal
- **Organization**: Make any remaining changes to organization and people
- **Accountability**: Hold leaders accountable and give them support and challenge
- **Operating model**: Refine your operating model and measurement and review approaches
- **Feedback**: Get formal feedback on role modeling for yourself and your team

A YEAR into her role, not everything had gone according to plan. Unforeseen changes in the economic climate had dictated a shift in strategy to focus more on the consumer business. She'd also had to move out another of her top team members unexpectedly after major risk and compliance issues had surfaced in his area. However, thanks to the operating rhythm Sofia had put in place, the team was able to pick up the need for adjustments at an early stage and make changes in a timely manner. As a result, the business unit was starting to see a turnaround in its performance. It had beaten its plan by delivering significant increases in cross-sell penetration and profit margins. In addition, 95 percent of employees now felt there was a clear, shared direction, up from less than 50 percent prior to Sofia's arrival. Most importantly, Sofia felt confident she had the right strategy, the right team, and the right support from stakeholders in place to keep moving forward.

LEADERSHIP TRANSITIONS:
AT A GLANCE

WHY IS IT IMPORTANT?

- Leadership transitions are high-stakes events.
- Nearly half of transitions fail, mostly due to the soft stuff.
- Transition frequency is rising, yet little help is on offer.

WHAT ARE THE BIG IDEAS?

- Take stock and take action in five areas simultaneously.
- Be as clear on what you won't do as what you will.
- Forget "100 days"—be impact-driven, not calendar-driven.

HOW DO I MAKE IT HAPPEN?

- Follow a five-step process to successfully transition.

  Most commonly neglected action in each step:

  Aspire: Co-create the aspiration with your team.

  Assess: Act early on "no regret" changes.

  Architect: Create a powerful, integrated change story.

  Act: Put in place "no surprises" review mechanisms.

  Advance: Ensure reflection/renewal time is set aside.

NOW WHAT?

SO THAT'S IT THEN. We've covered the ten most timeless topics—topics vital to any leader in any organization to get right, whether many years ago, today, or many years from now. For each, we've shared the business case for why they matter today as much as ever. We've suggested a short-list of research and experience-backed "big ideas" as to what you can do as a leader to capture the value at stake. Finally, we've provided a roadmap (and related case study) for how to apply the ideas in practice. Mission accomplished...

...Except for the fact that if we left it there, we'd be violating the very premise on which we decided to write this book! Leaders are busier than ever, hence the need for a one-stop shop of answers to perennial leadership questions. To leave you with a list of ten significant change programs on top of your already full leadership plate is hardly helpful! Indeed, there is one more question that must be addressed—in a world of constrained time and resources—where should I start?

The most straightforward answer for leaders as to where to start is to a) determine the relative importance of the topics covered in order to deliver your business strategy, and b) assess the effectiveness of your current organization for each topic. Where the biggest gaps are (e.g. high strategic importance and today's approach is not effective), that's a good place to start. The worksheet that follows—drawing on the big ideas we've shared on each topic—can help. To get the most value out of the exercise, we suggest also giving it to your team to complete, and then discuss the extent to which there is alignment, why, and what to do about it.

How important
is being best in
class on this topic
to your strategy?
1 = somewhat
2 = very
3 = extremely

What is our
Current state?
1 = best in class
2 = good
3 = not good

Priority index
(higher number is
higher priority)

1. Talent attraction and retention:	☐ A		AxE= F ☐

- We know which 5% of roles deliver 95% of the value ☐ B
- We have a magnetic offer, and are delivering on it ☐ C
- We are investing in technology as the next game-changer ☐ D

B+C+D= E ☐

2. Talent development:	☐ A		AxE= G ☐

- Our approach creates learning journeys that go far beyond the classroom and the computer ☐ B
- Our approach makes it personal for participants ☐ C
- Our approach is focused on an individual's strengths and is linked to stretch goals ☐ D

B+C+D= E ☐

3. Performance management:	☐ A		AxE= H ☐

- Our approach harmonizes company and employee motives ☐ B
- Our approach is seen as a fair process by all involved ☐ C
- We are more concerned with building the right skills than we are about systems and data ☐ D

B+C+D= E ☐

How important is being best in class on this topic to your strategy?
1 = somewhat
2 = very
3 = extremely

What is our **Current state?**
1 = best in class
2 = good
3 = not good

Priority index (higher number is higher priority)

---

4. High-performing teams: ☐ A AxE= I ☐

- We actively measure and manage our alignment, interaction, and renewal ☐ B

- Our team is focused on doing only the work that we can do ☐ C

- We don't let structure dictate who is on the team—it's the right people to deliver our strategy ☐ D

B+C+D= E ☐

---

5. Decision-making: ☐ A AxE= J ☐

- We differentiate among three types of decisions and adjust our approach accordingly ☐ B

- We treat dialogue as important as data and analytics ☐ C

- We effectively guard against biases ☐ D

B+C+D= E ☐

---

6. Organization design: ☐ A AxE= K ☐

- Our design addresses people, process, and structure, not just lines and boxes ☐ B

- We have both a stable backbone and agile elements in our design ☐ C

- We have followed the nine golden rules of a successful redesign process ☐ D

B+C+D= E ☐

How important
is being best in
class on this topic
to your strategy?
1 = somewhat
2 = very
3 = extremely

What is our
Current state?
1 = best in class
2 = good
3 = not good

Priority index
(higher number is
higher priority)

7. Overhead cost reduction: ☐ A — AxE= L ☐

- We take a zero-based approach ☐ B

- We fully apply the seven levers available to us ☐ C

- We have "fit for purpose" spans and layers (and not oversimplified) ☐ D

B+C+D= E ☐

8. Culture change: ☐ A — AxE= M ☐

- We focus on the nine elements that drive performance, not just engagement ☐ B

- We explicitly identify and shift underlying mindsets and behaviors ☐ C

- We employ the four high-impact levers to get the job done ☐ D

B+C+D= E ☐

9. Transformational change: ☐ A — AxE= N ☐

- We put equal time and effort into performance and health ☐ B

- We apply the "Five Frames" approach to transformational change ☐ C

- We are rational about how to fully leverage predictable irrationality ☐ D

B+C+D= E ☐

	How important is being best in class on this topic to your strategy? 1 = somewhat 2 = very 3 = extremely	What is our **Current state?** 1 = best in class 2 = good 3 = not good	**Priority index** (higher number is higher priority)

10. Leadership transitions:	☐ A		AxE= O ☐
· I purposefully take stock and action in five areas simultaneously		☐ B	
· I am as clear on what I and the company won't do as what I and we will		☐ C	
· I am impact-driven vs. calendar-driven		☐ D	
		B+C+D= E ☐	

Prioritization Summary

Topic	Priority index (from previous pages)	Priority ranking (rate 1 through 10, 1 being the highest priority index)	Notes
1. Talent attraction and retention	F		
2. Talent development	G		
3. Performance management	H		
4. High-performing teams	I		
5. Decision-making	J		
6. Organization design	K		
7. Overhead cost reduction	L		
8. Culture change	M		
9. Transformational change	N		
10. Leadership transitions	O		

This prioritization method is admittedly basic, reductionist, and mechanistic. In that regard, it could be likened to classic Newtonian physics. A more sophisticated view would be the equivalent of sub-atomic physics and not just at the level of each of the parts, but also how the parts dynamically interact with one another.

We've explored this arena, leveraging our database of over three million survey responses from over 1,500 organizations around the world. Those interested in the details should consult chapters two and three of Scott Keller and Colin Price's book, *Beyond Performance*, as the findings—like those of special relativity and wave particle duality in quantum physics – aren't easily summarized. The takeaway for leaders, however, is that you shouldn't try to be great at everything (e.g. trying to get your organization to be the General Electric of leadership development, the Apple of shaping the market, the Toyota of lean execution, and the Goldman Sachs of attracting top talent will make you mediocre at best). Instead, make explicit choices about the management practices in which nothing less than great will do, and where good enough is good enough.

That said, we'd point out that even though Newton's relatively simple equations don't hold under all conditions, they do a pretty good job in explaining our day-to-day reality!

For every timeless topic we've covered, there are no doubt multiple timely topics for which leaders would like to have a cut-through view of the business case (why), helpful insights (what), and guidance as to how to move the needle in practice (how). Examples of such topics include how to: increase diversity and inclusion, digitally transform, manage millennials, master compliance burdens, create more dynamic partnerships, and so on. In this context, we hope you'll see this as the end of the beginning of your journey with us—we'd love to engage with you about your questions, the answers you've developed, and simply hear your feedback on what you've read. We can be reached on the web at www.mckinsey.com/LeadingOrganizations or feel free to contact us at any time at scott_keller@mckinsey.com and mary_meaney@mckinsey.com. Until then, in the words of NASA's mission control to Apollo 11 as it embarked on its historic journey: "Good luck, and Godspeed."[1]

ACKNOWLEDGEMENTS

"WHO YOU GONNA CALL?" is the infectious refrain from Ray Parker Jr.'s soundtrack to the Hollywood supernatural comedy, *Ghostbusters*. When we were faced with that question in relation to the topic areas we've covered, we reached out to many of the leaders and members of McKinsey's Global Organization and Leadership Practice. Truth be told, this content is more theirs than ours! We've listed the experts that we've drawn on for each topic by region at www.mckinsey.com/LeadingOrganizations. Any of these leaders would glad to be your answer to "Who you gonna call?" to find out more.

We also particularly want to acknowledge two of our colleagues, Anita Baggio and Seham Husain, for their hands-on work in helping us pull together the content for this book. Similarly, without the support and guidance from the team at Bloomsbury, in particular Ian Hallsworth and Louise Tucker, this would never have made it into your hands in such an easy-to-read and engaging format. A special shoutout as well to Noah Smith and his team at Scrap Labs for designing the look and feel and bringing their creativity to the infographics.

Further, we are forever grateful to our families for putting up with the many weekends and late nights that had to be sacrificed to make this book a reality. Last but not least, we want YOU to know how much we appreciate your having joined us on this leg of the journey, and we welcome the opportunity to meet you on the next!

REFERENCES

FOREWORD

1 Jeffrey Pfeffer and Robert I. Sutton. *Hard Facts, Dangerous Half-Truths, and Total Nonsense: Profiting from Evidence-Based Management* (Cambridge, MA: Harvard Business Press, 2006), p. 45.
2 Jeffrey Pfeffer and Robert I. Sutton. *Hard Facts, Dangerous Half-Truths, and Total Nonsense: Profiting from Evidence-Based Management* (Cambridge, MA: Harvard Business Press, 2006), p. 29.
3 Will Schutz, *Profound Simplicity* (San Francisco: Pfeiffer & Company, 1982), p 54.

INTRODUCTION

1 https://next.ft.com/content/907fe3a6-1ce3-11e6-b286-cddde55ca122 Virtual memory: the race to save the information age by Richard Ovenden, May 19, 2016
2 http://www.mckinsey.com/business-functions/organization/our-insights/how-to-beat-the-transformation-odds

CHAPTER 1

1 Resch Group (2016), "Applying LEAN (and Elements of Six Sigma) for Process Optimization," (can be found at http://www.reschgroup.com/training/applying-lean-for-process-optimization/).
2 Ernest O'Boyle Jr. and Herman Aguinis, "The Best and the Rest: Revisiting the Norm of Normality in Individual Performance." *Personal Psychology*, 65 (2012): 79-119.
3 http://www.usatoday.com/story/money/personalfinance/2015/10/24/24-7-wallst- most-profitable-companies/74501312/
4 Kathleen Quinn Votaw, "How Steve Jobs got the A+ players and kept them," October 31, 2011. Can be found at talenttrust.com
5 Jim Collins, *Good to Great* (New York: Random House, 2001).
6 http://www.mckinsey.com/global-themes/employment-and-growth/talenttensions-ahead-a-ceo-briefing
7 Reference to graphic. McKinsey War for Talent, extensive research conducted 1997– 2000; survey of more than 12,000 executives at 125 midsize and large companies.

8   McKinsey & Company and The Conference Board, "The State of Human Capital 2012."
9   http://www.gallup.com/poll/188144/employee-engagement-stagnant- 2015.aspx
10 https://appirio.com/cloud-powered-blog/this-year-in-employee-engagement-2016-trends-to-watch
11 http://www.forbes.com/sites/jeannemeister/2012/08/14/job-hopping-is-the-new-normal-for-millennials-three-ways-to-prevent-ahuman-resource-nightmare/#2c9e516c5508
12 http://insight.kellogg.northwestern.edu/article/five-ways-to-attract-and-retain-data-scientists
13 http://www.forbes.com/sites/susanadams/2012/01/23/trust-in-ceos-plummets-but-still-beats-trust-in-government/#5459c4e8295f
14 http://www.bloomberg.com/news/articles/2015-11-17/machines-are-better-than-humans-at-hiring-top-employees
15 https://hbr.org/2014/05/in-hiring-algorithms-beat-instinct
16 http://dupress.com/articles/people-analytics-in-hr-analytics-teams/

CHAPTER 2

1   August Kerber, *Quotable Quotes on Education*, (Detroit: Wayne State University Press, 1968), p. 138. Reported as unverified in *Suzy Platt (ed.), Respectfully Quoted: A Dictionary of Quotations* (Washington D.C.: Library of Congress, 1989).
2   http://blogs.edweek.org/edweek/education_futures/2015/08/10_reasons_the_us_education_system_is_failing.html
3   The U.S. ranked 3 in the 2016 Best Countries for Education study conducted by the Wharton School of the University of Pennsylvania for U.S. News & World Report. http://www.usnews.com/news/best-countries/education-full-list; The Nations Social Progress Index basic education rating (which takes out the weight of the higher education system in the U.S.) rates the U.S. in the top 15 of 196 countries in the world. http://www.mbctimes.com/english/20-best-education-systems-world
4   http://www.mckinsey.com/global-themes/employment-and-growth/future-of-work-in-advanced-economies
5   Pankaj Ghemawat, "Developing global leaders," *McKinsey Quarterly, 2012.*
6   McKinsey & Company and The Conference Board, "The State of Human Capital 2012."
7   http://www.lhh.com/press-room/news/investments-in-leadership-development-to-increase
8   https://www.ziglar.com/quotes/employees/
9   http://www.gallup.com/businessjournal/182228/managers-engaged-jobs.aspx
10 http://www.economist.com/news/business/21651217-more-firms-have-set-up-their-own-corporate-universities-they-have-become-less-willing-pay
11 http://dupress.com/articles/learning-and-development-human-capital-trends-2015/; http://www.bersin.com/corporate-learning-factbook-2014
12 "The Corporate Learning Factbook 2014: Benchmarks, Trends, and Analysis of the U.S. Training Market", January 2014, Bersin.
13 http://www.mckinsey.com/global-themes/leadership/why-leadership-developmentprograms-fail; original source is Matthew Gitsham, *Developing the Global Leader of Tomorrow* (Ashridge, 2009).

14 http://www.forbes.com/sites/joshbersin/2014/02/04/the-recovery-arrives-corporate-training-spend-skyrockets/#5362bf394ab7

15 https://www.washingtonpost.com/news/on-leadership/wp/2014/09/05/what-employers-really-want-workers-they-dont-have-to-train/

16 https://www.shrm.org/resourcesandtools/tools-and-samples/toolkits/pages developingemployeecareerpathsandladders.aspx

17 http://www.businessnewsdaily.com/7366-no-career-roadmap.html#sthash.kjm1YrIV.dpuf

18 http://www.ncbi.nlm.nih.gov/pubmed/11894680

19 http://www.bostoncommons.net/knowledge-doubling/

20 Research from *Lessons of Experience* (Lexington Press, 1988), later summarized in *Career Architect Planner* (Lominger Press, 1996).

21 McKinsey & Company Human Capital Service Line research, 2014.

22 Rachel Emma Silverman, "So Much Training, So Little to Show for It", *Wall Street Journal*, October 26, 2012.

23 http://www.gse.upenn.edu/news/press-releases/penn-gse-study-shows-moocs-have-relatively-few-active-users-only-few-persisting-

24 Ola Svenson, "Are we all less risky and more skillful than our fellow drivers?", *Acta Psychologica*, 47 (1981): 143–148.

25 Mark D. Alicke and Olesya Govorun, "The better-than-average effect," in Mark D. Alicke, David A. Dunning and Joachim I. Krueger, *The Self in Social Judgment: Studies in Self and Identity* (Hove: Psychology Press, 2005), 85–106.

26 Michael Ross and Fiore Sicoly, "Egocentric Biases in Availability and Attribution," *Journal of Personality and Social Psychology*, 37 (1979): 322–336; http://psych.colorado.edu/~vanboven/teaching/p7536_heurbias/p7536_readings/rosssicoly1979.pdf

27 http://www.gordontraining.com/free-workplace-articles/learning-a-new-skill-is-easier-said-than-done/

28 http://www.gallup.com/businessjournal/153341/why-strengths-matter-training.aspx

29 "Return on Leadership": joint study by Egon Zehnder International and McKinsey & Company, February 2011.

30 Claudio Fernández-Aráoz, "21st-Century Talent Spotting," *Harvard Business Review*, June 2014 (accessed online).

CHAPTER 3

1 http://pages.stern.nyu.edu/~wstarbuc/ChinCtrl.html

2 Kevin Murphy and Jeanette N. Cleveland, *Understanding Performance Appraisal: Social, Organizational, and Goal-Based Perspectives* (New York: Sage Publications, 2005).

3 W. R. Spriegel, (1962), "Company practices in appraisal of managerial performance," *Personnel Journal*, Vol. 39: 77–83.

4 http://www.ysc.com/our-thinking/article/the-end-of-performance-management-sorting-the-facts-from-the-hype

5 John C. Maxwell, *The 360 Degree Leader: Developing Your Influence from Anywhere in the Organization* (New York: Thomas Nelson publishing, 2005).

6 P. Drucker, *The Practice of Management* (Harper, New York, 1954); Heinemann, London, 1955; revised edn, Butterworth-Heinemann, 2007.

7   J. E. Hunter and Robert Rodgers, "Impact of management by objectives on organizational productivity," *J. Appl. Psychol.*, 76 (1991): 322–336.

8   S. Wagner, C. P. Parker, N. Christiansen, "Employees that think and act like owners: Effects of ownership beliefs and behaviors on organizational effectiveness," *Personnel Psychology*, 56 (2003): 847–871.

9   Deborah Brecher, Johan Eerenstein, Catherine Farley, and Good, Tim, "Is performance management performing,"Accenture (2016).

10 https://hbr.org/2015/03/why-strategy-execution-unravelsand-what-to-do-about-it

11 The Conference Board CEO Challenge 2015 "Creating Opportunity out of Adversity—Building Innovative, People-Driven Organizations," by Charles Mitchell, Rebecca Ray, Bart van Ark.

12 Brecher, Deborah, Eerenstein, Johan, Farley, Catherine, and Good, Tim (April 2016), "Is performance management performing," Accenture.

13 2013 Global Performance Management Survey Report by Mercer.

14 https://www.washingtonpost.com/news/on-leadership/wp/2015/07/21/in-big-move-accenture-will-get-rid-of-annual-performance-reviews-and-rankings/

15 Daniel H. Pink, *Drive* (New York: Riverhead Books, 2011).

16 https://www.boundless.com/psychology/textbooks/boundless-psychology-textbook/motivation-12/theories-of-motivation-65/incentive-theory-of-motivation-and-intrinsic-vs-extrinsic-motivation- 252-12787/

17 Daniel H. Pink, *Drive* (New York: Riverhead Books, 2011).

18 https://www.psychologytoday.com/blog/old-school-parenting-modern-day-families/201505/the-failure-child-centered-parenting

19 Terry Burnham and Jay Phelan, *Mean Genes* (New York: Perseus, 2000).

20 http://www.wsj.com/news/articles/SB10001424052970203363504577186970064375222

21 https://www.shrm.org/ResourcesAndTools/hr-topics/employee-relations/Pages/performance-reviews-are-dead.aspx

22 https://www.cebglobal.com/blogs/corporate-hr-removing-performance-ratings-is-unlikely-to-improve-performance/

CHAPTER 4

1   http://www.forbes.com/sites/erikaandersen/2013/05/31/21-quotes-from-henry-ford-on-business-leadership-and-life/#6aeca8443700

2   http://articles.latimes.com/1992-06-25/sports/sp-1411_1_olympic-team

3   http://thegrio.com/2012/06/13/dream-team-documentarys-5-most-intriguing-moments/

4   http://worldsoccertalk.com/2014/07/14/why-germany-won-the-world-cup-and-why-they-may-not-be-perfect/

5   https://www.entrepreneur.com/article/241441

6   Global Institutional Investor survey, Ernst & Young 2009.

7   Scott Keller and Colin Price, *Beyond Performance: How Great Organizations Build Ultimate Competitive Advantage* (Hoboken, N.J.: Wiley, 2011).

8   https://www.sciencedaily.com/releases/2006/04/060423191907.htm

9   https://www.entrepreneur.com/article/269941

10 http://www.inc.com/dave-kerpen/15-quotes-to-inspire-great-team-work.html

11 Kenwyn K. Smith and David N. Berg, *Paradoxes of Group Life* (San Francisco: Jossey-Bass Inc, 1987).

12 Research jointly conducted by Leadership Consulting practice of executive search firm Heidrick & Struggles and University of Southern California's Center for Effective Organization with 60 top HR Executives from Fortune 500 companies; Richard M. Rosen and Fred Adair, "CEOs misperceive top teams' performance," *Harvard Business Review*, September 2007.

13 Diane Cotu, "Why teams don't work," *Harvard Business Review*, May 2009.

14 Richard M. Rosen and Fred Adair, "CEOs misperceive top teams' performance," *Harvard Business Review*, September 2007.

15 Original source: PwC's 18th Annual Global CEO Survey 2015 http://www.pwc.com/gx/en/ceo-survey/2015/assets/pwc-18th-annual-global-ceo-survey-jan-2015.pdf

16 http://www.cnn.com/2010/BUSINESS/03/12/ceo.health.warning/

17 http://www.brainyquote.com/quotes/keywords/dream.html

18 http://www.nytimes.com/2016/02/28/magazine/what-google-learned-from-its-quest-to-build-the-perfect-team.html?_r=0

19 Original source: Senior Leadership Teams: What It Takes to Make Them Great (Center for Public Leadership) Hardcover – January 24, 2008. Ruth Wageman, Debra Nunes, James Burruss, and Richard Hackman collected and analyzed data on more than 120 top teams around the world; published at "Why Teams Don't Work,"—*Harvard Business Review* https://hbr.org/2009/05/why-teams-dont-work

20 "Why Teams Don't Work," *Harvard Business Review* https://hbr.org/2009/05/why-teams-dont-work

CHAPTER 5

1   Leigh Buchanan and Andrew O'Connell, "A Brief History of Decision-Making," *Harvard Business Review*, January 2006.

2   http://go.roberts.edu/leadingedge/the-great-choices-of-strategic-leaders

3   Leigh Buchanan and Andrew O'Connell, "A Brief History of Decision-Making," *Harvard Business Review*, January 2006.

4   http://www.nytimes.com/2008/05/02/technology/02kodak.html

5   Marcia W. Blenko, Michael C. Mankins and Paul Rogers, "The decision-driven organization," *Harvard Business Review*, June 2010.

6   Dan Lovallo and Olivier Sibony, "The case for behavioral strategy," *McKinsey Quarterly*, March 2010.

7   Our analysis leverages additional source data from http://www.bain.com/publications/articles/the-five-steps-to-better-decisions.aspx

8   Towers Perrin Global Workforce Survey 2007–2008.

9   http://knowledge.wharton.upenn.edu/article/a-tale-of-two-brands-yahoos-mistakes-vs-googles-mastery/

10 Amir Efrati "Yahoo Battles Brain Drain," *Wall Street Journal*, December 5, 2011.

11 Cyril Northcote Parkinson, *Parkinson's Law, or The Pursuit of Progress* (London: John Murray, 1958).

12 Dan Ariely, Interview by Olivier Sibony, *McKinsey Quarterly*, 2011.

13 http://www.mckinsey.com/business-functions/strategy-and-corporate-finance/our-insights/the-case-for-behavioral-strategy

14 https://blog.deming.org/w-edwards-deming-quotes/large-list-of-quotes-by-w-edwards-deming/

15 "A Victim of Its Own Success," *Financial Times*, April 4, 2012.
16 http://www.information-age.com/industry/uk-industry/296791/kodak-presses-the-digital-switch
17 Bent Flyvbjerg, Mette Skamris Holm, and Soren Buhl, "How common and how large are cost overruns in transport infrastructure projects?" *Transport Reviews*, 23 (2003): 71-88.
18 "Dan Ariely on Irrationality in the Workplace," *McKinsey Quarterly*, February 2011.
19 Data from: http://www.nytimes.com/2015/12/09/opinion/diversity-makes-you-brighter.html?_r=0, other similar studies include http://insight.kellogg.northwestern.edu/article/better_decisions_through_diversity, https://www.gsb.stanford.edu/insights/deborah-gruenfeld-diverse-teams-produce-better-decisions,

CHAPTER 6

1   Frederic Laloux, *Reinventing Organizations: A Guide to Creating Organizations Inspired by the Next Stage in Human Consciousness* (Nelson Parker: Brussels, 2014).
2   https://www.gsb.stanford.edu/insights/jeffrey-pfeffer-do-workplace-hierarchiesstill-matter, http://www.inc.com/christina-desmarais/your-employees-likehierarchy-no-really.html
3   Chris Morgan and David Langford, *Facts and Fallacies: A Book of Definitive Mistakes and Misguided Predictions* (New York: St Martin's Press, 1981).
4   McKinsey Global Survey results; The secrets of successful organizational redesigns, September 10 to September 20, 2013, garnered responses from 2,063 executives representing the full range of regions, industries, company sizes, functional specialties, and tenures. Of those, 1,534 say they have experienced a redesign at their current organizations.
5   http://www.eremedia.com/ere/survey-says-executive-tenure-shortening/
6   http://chiefexecutive.net/why-ceos-are-taking-on-more-direct-reports
7   http://www.forbes.com/2010/07/30/corporate-reorganization-abb-fordleadership-managing-bain.html
8   "How do I reorganize to capture maximum value quickly?" McKinsey Organization Practice white paper, Giancarlo Ghislanzoni, Stephen Heidari-Robinson, Suzanne Heywood, Martin Jermiin, November 2011.
9   https://hbr.org/2014/01/five-questions-every-leader-should-ask-about organizational-design?utm_source=feedburner&utm_medium=feed&utm_campaign=Feed %3A+harvardbusiness+%28HBR.org%29
10 McKinsey Global Survey results, The secrets of successful organizational redesigns, September 10 to September 20, 2013, and garnered responses from 2,063 executives representing the full range of regions, industries, company sizes, functional specialties, and tenures. Of those, 1,534 say they have experienced a redesign at their current organizations. Numbers add to over 100 as most reorganizations have multiple objectives.
11 Phil Rosenzweig, *The Halo Effect: How Managers let Themselves be Deceived* (New York: Free Press, 2007).
12 Phil Rosenzweig, *The Halo Effect: How Managers let Themselves be Deceived* (New York: Free Press, 2007).
13 Dan Bilefsky and Anita Raghavan, "Once Called 'Europe's GE,' ABB and Star CEO Tumbled," *Wall Street Journal*, January 23, 2003.

14 A quote by Charlton Ogburn (1911–1998) in "Merrill's Marauders: The truth about an incredible adventure" in the January 1957 issue of *Harper's Magazine*. Ogburn wrote two distinct but similar versions. One was printed in *Harper's Magazine* in January 1957 and the other appeared in his memoir *The Marauders*, 1959.

15 McKinsey Global Survey results, The secrets of successful organizational redesigns, September 2013. We note that the data reported in the initial report differs slightly to what we report here because on a review of the base data we found that there were 103 cases that, upon further analysis, we considered ambiguous as they were still in implementation. The variance in numbers is accounted for by taking these cases out of the data set (making N=1208).

16 IBS Center for Management Research, 2003.

17 http://allthingsd.com/20090209/will-tough-talking-bartz-reorg-yahoo-soon-andfinally-blue-pill-the-matrix/

18 http://www.webmd.com/back-pain/news/20140325/low-back-pain-leadingcause-of-disability-worldwide-study

19 http://www.smi-mindbodyresearch.org/Schechter2Web.pdf

20 John E. Sarno, MD, *Healing Back Pain: The Mind-Body Connection* (New York: Warner Books, 1991).

21 http://www.nbcnews.com/id/39658423/ns/health-pain_center/t/back-surgerymay-backfire-patients-pain/#.V-OMY_krJhQ

22 John E. Sarno, MD, *Healing Back Pain: The Mind-Body Connection* (New York: Warner Books, 1991).

23 "How the Growth Outliers Do It", *Harvard Business Review*, January–February 2012.

24 Carlos Ruiz Zafón, *The Angel's Game* (London: Weidenfeld & Nicolson, 2009)

25 Steven Aronowitz, Aaron De Smet and Deirdre McGinty, "Getting organizational redesign right", *McKinsey Quarterly*, June 2015.

CHAPTER 7

1 Joseph A. Tainter, *The Collapse of Complex Societies*, New Studies in Archaeology (Cambridge: CUP, 1988).

2 Edward Gibbon, *The History of the Decline and Fall of the Roman Empire* (1776).

3 Bobbie Gossage, "Howard Schultz on how to lead a turnaround," *Inc. Magazine*, April 2011.

4 Robert Levin and Alison Watson, "Maximizing the value of G&A," *McKinsey Quarterly*, June 2016.

5 Chris Bradley, Angus Dawson and Sven Smit, "The strategic yardstick you can't afford to ignore," *McKinsey Quarterly*, October 2013.

6 http://www.pwc.com/gx/en/ceo-survey/2016/landing-page/pwc-19th-annualglobal-ceo-survey.pdf

7 http://www.mckinsey.com/business-functions/operations/our-insights/whatworked-in-cost-cutting-and--and-whats-next-mckinsey-global-survey-results

8 Alexander Edlich, Heiko Heimes and Alison Watson Pugh, "Can you achieve and sustain your G&A cost reductions?" *McKinsey Quarterly*, October 2016.

9 http://www.bain.com/Images/BAIN_BRIEF_Break_out_from_the_G_and_A_cost_treadmill.pdf

10 Suzanne P., Nimocks, Robert L. Rosiello, and Oliver Wright, "Managing overhead costs," *McKinsey Quarterly*, May 2005.
11 2013 Global Burden of Disease Study https://www.nielsen.com/content/dam/nielsenglobal/eu/nielseninsights/pdfs/Nielsen%20Global%20Health%20and%20Wellness%20Report%20-%20January%202015.pdf
12 Gary Foster, Ph.D., clinical director of the Weight and Eating Disorders Program at the University of Pennsylvania, http://www.livestrong.com/article/438395-thepercentage-of-people-who-regain-weight-after-rapid-weight-loss-risks/
13 http://www.livestrong.com/article/438395-the-percentage-of-people-who-regainweight-after-rapid-weight-loss-risks/
14 https://www.pacifichealthlabs.com/blog/could-you-be-losing-muscle-instead-offat-heres-how-not-to-do-that/
15 Brian Hackett, "Cut the costs, but not the trust," The Conference Board, 2002.
16 https://hbr.org/2008/05/halting-the-exodus-after-a-layoff
17 http://www.compensationforce.com/2016/04/2015-turnover-rates-by-industry.html
18 https://www.zanebenefits.com/blog/bid/312123/employee-retention-the-realcost- of-losing-an-employee
19 This vignette draws on an Internet meme that has no discernable originator. The authors were inspired by the version of the meme written in Raymond S. Edge and John Randall Groves, *Ethics of Health Care: A Guide for Clinical Practice*, (New York: Thomson Delmar Learning, 1994).
20 http://disenthrall.co/3-examples-of-the-anchoring-rule-in-marketing/
21 Shaun Callaghan, Kyle Hawke and Carey Mignerey, "Five myths (and realities) about zero-based budgeting," *McKinsey Quarterly*, October 2014.
22 https://www.bcgperspectives.com/content/articles/organization_design_public_sector_demystifying_organization_design_in_the_public_sector/
23 Julie Wulf, "The Flattened Firm—Not As Advertised", Working Paper 12-087, Harvard Business School, April 9, 2012.

CHAPTER 8

1 http://www.micsem.org/pubs/counselor/frames/culture_economic_developmentfr.htm?http&&&www.micsem.org/pubs/counselor/culture_economic_development.htm drawing on *Principles of Political Economy* (1848) by John Stuart Mill and *Protestant Ethic and the Theory of Capitalism* by Max Weber
2 David Landes, *The Wealth and Poverty of Nations* (New York: W.W. Norton, 1998).
3 J. P. Kotter and J. L. Heskett, *Corporate Culture and Performance* (New York: Free Press, 1992).
4 Scott Keller and Colin Price, *Beyond Performance: How Great Organizations Build Ultimate Competitive Advantage* (Hoboken, N.J.: Wiley, 2011).
5 Dan M. Kahan, Ellen Peters, Erica Cantrell Dawson, and Paul Slovic, "Motivated Numeracy and Enlightened Self-Government," *Behavioural Public Policy*, Forthcoming; Yale Law School, Public Law Working Paper No. 307, September 3, 2013.
6 Gary Hamel and C. K. Prahalad *Competing for the Future* (Boston: Harvard Business School Press, 1996).

7   http://www.slideshare.net/reed2001/culture-1798664, 2009.

8   Chris DeRose and Noel Tichy "Judgement is All: does JCPenney's Ron Johnson fatally lack it?" *Forbes*, March 8, 2013.

9   https://www.torbenrick.eu/blog/culture/organisational-culture-eats-strategy-forbreakfast-lunch-and-dinner/

10 Patricia Sellers "Warren Buffet, corporate culture guru," *Fortune Magazine*, March 17, 2011.

11 Scott Keller and Colin Price, *Beyond Performance: How Great Organizations Build Ultimate Competitive Advantage* (Hoboken, N.J.: Wiley, 2011).

12 http://www.bloomberg.com/news/articles/2003-03-30/an-insiders-tale-ofenrons-toxic-culture

13 http://www.independent.co.uk/news/business/news/exclusive-barclays-insiderlifts-lid-on-banks-toxic-culture-7920809.html

14 Scott Keller and Colin Price, *Beyond Performance: How Great Organizations Build Ultimate Competitive Advantage* (Hoboken, N.J.: Wiley, 2011).

15 http://www.telegraph.co.uk/finance/newsbysector/industry/engineering/12043637/Misconduct-at-heart-of-VWs-dieselgate-scandal-sayschairman.html

16 Scott Keller and Colin Price, *Beyond Performance: How Great Organizations Build Ultimate Competitive Advantage* (Hoboken, N.J.: Wiley, 2011).

17 http://www.fastcompany.com/1810674/culture-eats-strategy-lunch

18 Lou Gerstner, *Who Says Elephants Can't Dance?* (New York: HarperBusiness, 2002).

19 Scott Keller and Colin Price, *Beyond Performance: How Great Organizations Build Ultimate Competitive Advantage* (Hoboken, N.J.: Wiley, 2011).

20 R. E. Ulrich, "The use of behavior modification strategies to increase the probability of attendance at evening chapel through the use of food contingent reinforcement at the Life Line Mission, San Francisco, California," *Behaviorists for Social Action Journal*, 2 (1980): 1–2.

21 Scott Keller and Colin Price, *Beyond Performance: How Great Organizations Build Ultimate Competitive Advantage* (Hoboken, N.J.: Wiley, 2011).

CHAPTER 9

1   John F. Kennedy's "Address in the Assembly Hall at the Paulskirche in Frankfurt., June 25, 1963", as reported by http://www.presidency.ucsb.edu/ws/?pid=9303

2   Kurt Lewin, "Frontiers in Group Dynamics: concept, method and reality in social science; social equilibria and social change," *Human Relations*, Vol 1, 1947, 5–41. http://dx.doi.org/10.1177/001872674700100103.

3   Joel Barker, Brad Christensen, John Christensen, and Charthouse Learning Corporation, *The Power of Vision* (VHS: Burnsville, MN, 1990).

4   Andreas Cornet, Philipp Espel and Daniel Hannemann, "On Enterprise Transformations," McKinsey & Company Organization Practice white paper, February 2016.

5   "Introduction," Scott Keller and Colin Price, *Beyond Performance: How Great Organizations Build Ultimate Competitive Advantage* (Hoboken, N.J.: Wiley, 2011).

6   http://www.innosight.com/innovation-resources/strategy-innovation/creativedestruction-whips-through-corporate-america.cfm

7   http://www.theatlantic.com/business/archive/2015/05/lotteries-americas-70-billion-shame/392870/

8 http://www.iii.org/fact-statistic/mortality-risk
9 Martin E. Smith, "Success rates for different types of organizational change," *Performance Improvement* 41 (2002): 26–33.
10 http://www.mckinsey.com/business-functions/organization/our-insights/how-tobeat-the-transformation-odds
11 George M. Marsden, C. S. Lewis's *"Mere Christianity": A Biography* (Princeton University Press: Princeton N.J.: 2016).
12 Scott Keller and Colin Price, Beyond Performance: *How Great Organizations Build Ultimate Competitive Advantage* (Hoboken, N.J.: Wiley, 2011), p. 30.
13 George Johnson, Strange Beauty: *Murray Gell-Mann and the Revolution in Twentieth-Century Physics* (Vintage: New York, 1999).

CHAPTER 10

1 https://www.armstrongeconomics.com/writings/2012-2/anatomy-of-a-debt-crisis/
2 http://www.ddiworld.com/DDI/media/trend-research/leaders-in-transitionstepping-up-not-off_mis_ddi.pdf
3 Kruti Bharucha and Nitika Dial, "Corporate Finance: The Cost of Poor Leadership Transitions," CEB, October 29 2013; https://www.cebglobal.com/blogs/corporate-finance-the-cost-of-poor-leadership-transitions/
4 https://www.americanprogress.org/wp-content/uploads/2012/11/Costof Turnover.pdf
5 Brad Tuttle, "The 5 Big Mistakes That Led to Ron Johnson's Ouster at J.C. Penney," *Time*, April 9 2013; retrieved January 7 2015.
6 The statistics on failure rates and their causes have been compiled from a number of landmark studies, including: Brad Smart and Geoff Smart, *Topgrading: How to Hire, Coach and Keep A Players* (New York: Penguin, 1999); Mark Murphy, "Leadership IQ study: Why new hires fail," *Public Management*, 88 (2: 2005); "Executive transitions market study: Summary report 2008," Institute of Executive Development and Alexcel Group, 2008; George Bradt, Jayme Check, and Jorge Pedraza, *The New Leader's 100-Day Action Plan* (Hoboken N.J.: Wiley, 2009); and recent Gallup polls. The specific range mentioned here comes from Executive Transitions Rise, Challenges Continue, IED and Alexcel research June 2013 ("Today approximately 27 percent of executives fail to meet expectations in their first two years") and "High-impact leadership transitions: a transformative approach," CEB, 2012 ("46 percent of all leaders underperform during the course of their transitions").
7 Carolyn Dewar, Seham Husain and Scott Keller, "Breaking new ground: making a successful transition into your new executive role," McKinsey & Company, 2013.
8 http://mld.mckinsey.com/custom-program/leadership-transitions#.V9SXVfkrJzU
9 http://www.ddiworld.com/DDI/media/trend-research/leaders-in-transitionstepping-up-not-off_mis_ddi.pdf
10 Jennifer Reingold, "How to Fail in Business While Really, Really Trying," *Fortune*, March 20, 2014.
11 Phil Wahba, "Ron Johnson says JCPenney should have stuck to his plan," *Fortune*, May 16, 2016.
12 Jennifer Reingold, "How to Fail in Business While Really, Really Trying," *Fortune*, March 20, 2014.

13 Marshall Goldsmith with Mark Reiter, *What Got You Here – Won't Get You There* (New York: Hyperion, 2007).

14 PWC 2015 CEO Success study http://www.strategyand.pwc.com/ceosuccess

15 Michael Birshan, Thomas Meakin and Kurt Strovink, "How new CEOs can boost their odds of success," *McKinsey Quarterly*, May 2016.

16 Executive Transitions Rise, Challenges Continue, IED and Alexcel research June 2013.

17 Matt Paese, PhD and Richard Wellins, PhD, "Leaders in Transition: Stepping up, not off," (DDI) and Rajiv Chandran, Hortense de la Boutetiere and Carolyn Dewar, "Ascending to the C-suite," *McKinsey Quarterly*, April 2015.

18 CEB, "High-Impact Leadership Transitions," 2012: 8.

19 Patricia Wheeler PhD, "Executive transitions market study summary report: 2008," The Institute of Executive Development, 2008.

20 Rajiv Chandran, Hortense de la Boutetiere and Carolyn Dewar, "Ascending to the C-suite," *McKinsey Quarterly*, April 2015.

21 Executive Transitions Rise, Challenges Continue, IED and Alexcel research June 2013.

22 Michael Birshan, Thomas Meakin and Kurt Strovink, "How new CEOs can boost their odds of success," *McKinsey Quarterly*, May 2016.

23 Rajat Gupta and Jim Wendler, "Leading Change: An Interview with the CEO of P&G," *McKinsey Quarterly*, July 2005.

24 John Greathouse, "Steve Jobs: 5 (More) Motivational Business Tips," Forbes.com, May 18, 2013.

25 Debbie Weil, "Three things on Jim Collins' stop doing list," *Inc. Magazine*, September, 2008.

26 Rajiv Chandran, Hortense de la Boutetiere and Carolyn Dewar, "Ascending to the C-suite," *McKinsey Quarterly*, April 2015.

27 Patricia Wheeler PhD, "Executive transitions market study summary report: 2008," The Institute of Executive Development, 2008.

28 Leslie Gaines-Ross, *CEO Capital: A Guide to Building CEO Reputation and Company Success* (Hoboken, NJ: John Wiley & Sons, 2002).

29 Rajiv Chandran, Hortense de la Boutetiere and Carolyn Dewar, "Ascending to the C-suite," *McKinsey Quarterly*, April 2015.

30 https://www.fastcompany.com/53574/fast-company-interview-jeff-immelt

CHAPTER 11

1   http://www.scientificamerican.com/article/good-luck-and-godspeed/

INDEX